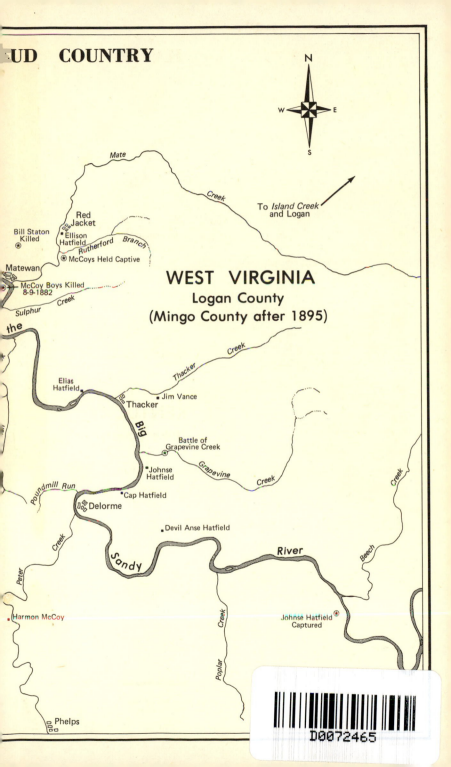

UD   COUNTRY

N
W   E
S

Mate

Creek

To *Island Creek*
and Logan

Red
Jacket

Bill Staton
Killed ⊛

Ellison
Hatfield

Rutherford   *Branch*

McCoys Held Captive ⊛

Matewan

McCoy Boys Killed
8-9-1882

Sulphur   Creek

the

WEST   VIRGINIA
Logan County
(Mingo County after 1895)

Thacker   Creek

Elias
Hatfield

Thacker

Jim Vance

Big

Battle of
Grapevine Creek

Johnse
Hatfield

Grapevine   Creek

Creek

Poundmill Run

Delorme

Cap Hatfield

Devil Anse Hatfield

River   Beech

Creek

Sandy

Peter

Harmon McCoy

Johnse Hatfield ⊛
Captured

Creek

Poplar

Phelps

The Hatfields
and
the McCoys

OTIS K. RICE

THE UNIVERSITY PRESS OF KENTUCKY

Endsheet map by CartoGraphics

Rice, Otis K
　　The Hatfields and the McCoys.

　　(The Kentucky Bicentennial bookshelf)
　　Includes bibliographical references.
　　1. Hatfield-McCoy feud.　I. Title.　II. Series.
HV6452.K42H35　1978　　　　975.4'48'04　　　　78-57388
ISBN 0-8131-0235-9

Research for The Kentucky Bicentennial Bookshelf
is assisted by a grant from the
National Endowment for the Humanities.
Views expressed in the Bookshelf do not
necessarily represent those of the Endowment.

A statewide cooperative scholarly publishing agency
serving Berea College, Centre College of Kentucky,
Eastern Kentucky University, The Filson Club,
Georgetown College, Kentucky Historical Society,
Kentucky State University, Morehead State University,
Murray State University, Northern Kentucky University,
Transylvania University, University of Kentucky,
University of Louisville, and Western Kentucky University.

Editorial and Sales Offices: Lexington, Kentucky 40506

TO MY SISTERS
Alma and Rosalie Rice

AND MY GRANDNEPHEW
David Neal Thomas

Contents

Preface

Without question, the Hatfield-McCoy feud has excited more interest than any of the late nineteenth-century vendettas of the southern Appalachian Mountains. Scores of books and articles have related its history, and novels, motion pictures, and outdoor dramas have drawn their inspiration from it. Unfortunately, too many of the depictions have been more given to sensationalism than to accuracy and objectivity.

At the outset, it must be recognized that the origins of the feud were complex and cannot be identified with one particular event. Moreover, many of the details of events in the feud may never be known with certainty, for accounts, even by participants, were often so contradictory that there is no way of determining precisely where the truth ended and fabrication began. In addition, many newspaper accounts were so biased or so grossly inaccurate that they must be used with considerable discrimination. Reminiscences in which long conversations were recalled verbatim, used by some writers, are by their very nature suspect.

The present study makes no claim to the discovery of the ultimate truth of every detail of the feud. I have tried, however, to separate myth from known facts, to present as dispassionate and balanced an account as available sources will afford, and to place the feud in the social, economic, political, and cultural context in which it occurred. I have drawn as much as possible from contemporary sources, including court records, public documents, and other materials, including newspapers, that offer a degree of reliability. Above all, I have sought to weigh evidence carefully and to avoid the partisanship and condescension that have characterized much of the writing on the feud.

In my research and writing I have incurred the usual debts that any author accumulates. As always, I have found librarians and their staffs ready to respond to my calls with the kind of assistance that only they can render. I must acknowledge special debts to Mr. William Marshall and the staff of the Special Collections of the University of Kentucky Library; Mr. Jeffrey M. Duff of the Kentucky Division of Archives and Records; Miss Linda Anderson of the Kentucky Historical Society; Mrs. Carol Warner of the West Virginia Department of Archives and History; and the staffs of the West Virginia Collection of the West Virginia University Library and the Vining Library of West Virginia Institute of Technology. Dr. Thomas D. Clark drew my attention to the collection of Pike County records in the University of Kentucky Library. My niece, Mrs. Martha Ellen Thomas, photocopied materials in the University of Kentucky Library. Leonard McCoy of Phelps, Kentucky, generously allowed me to use photographs in his possession, and Leonard W. Roberts kindly arranged with the Pike County Historical Society and the Preservation Council of Pike County, Inc., for others. My secretary, Mrs. Connie Alexander, assisted with the typing.

I especially appreciate a grant from the Research and Publications Committee of West Virginia Institute of Technology, which facilitated last-minute research. Two student assistants, Ray E. Woods, Jr., and David Hardy, assisted me in checking references and photocopying needed materials. My colleague Dr. Stephen W. Brown read the entire manuscript and, as usual, made a number of useful suggestions.

1

THE FEUDISTS AND
THEIR SOCIETY

A STORY CARRIED by numerous newspapers in June 1977 reported great agitation among residents of the eastern Kentucky town of Pikeville over a proposal to move the graves in the Dils Cemetery to make way for a civic center and sports arena. The outcry against what ordinarily might have seemed the march of progress arose from the fact that the cemetery provided the last resting-places of Randolph McCoy, his wife Sarah, and other members of the famous Kentucky feuding family. Some of the opponents of removal of the graves must have reasoned that those whose lives had known so little peace should be left undisturbed in death. As usual, many newspaper allusions to the famous vendetta contained gross errors, among them the assertion that more than one hundred men, women, and children were killed during the feud. Only in declaring that "the cause of the feud was never clear" did some of them get closer to the truth.[1]

Nearly a century has passed since the trouble between the Hatfields and the McCoys broke the quiet of the hills along the Kentucky-West Virginia border. When they finally laid aside their weapons, members of both families preferred to forget an ugly chapter in their history. In later years battle-scarred veterans of the feud seldom spoke of it. When they did reflect upon the troubles between the two families they often disagreed about their origins and details of the principal events.

Any serious study of the Hatfield-McCoy feud requires more than a mere retelling of the events which drew the conflict to national attention. Of considerable importance to an understanding of the vendetta are the characteristics and backgrounds of the two families, the nature of the environment in which they lived, the social mores of the Kentucky and West Virginia mountains, the prevailing economic patterns, the viability of political and social institutions, and even the impact of outside influences in perpetuating the feud once it started.

Let us begin with the land itself. The valley of the Tug Fork of the Big Sandy River, in which the feud occurred, is one of the most rugged and forbidding sections of the Appalachian Highlands. The Tug Fork draws its waters from scores of small tributaries that have carved deep, narrow valleys from the surrounding sandstone and limestone rocks. At Louisa, Kentucky, the Tug Fork joins the Levisa Fork to form the Big Sandy River proper, which, in turn, flows into the Ohio at Catlettsburg, Kentucky. Like much of the surrounding territory, the watershed of the Tug Fork consists of a maze of secluded valleys that long remained almost inaccessible, where men might live virtually undisturbed by outside influences. The river provided a geographical unity for the region, but, as the boundary between Kentucky and West Virginia, it divided it politically, thereby aggravating some of the conditions that nourished the Hatfield-McCoy feud.

The paths of men go everywhere, and by the beginning of the nineteenth century settlers, mostly from Montgomery, Washington, and Russell counties in southwestern Virginia, began to filter into the Tug Valley. Many of these pioneers claimed descent from Scottish stock, both Highland and Lowland, and were drawn from the great stream of European immigrants who reached American shores in the early eighteenth century and moved westward by way of the Valley of Virginia.

They bore such names as Hatfield, McCoy, Smith, Vance, Chafin, Cline, Evans, Weddington, Staton, Trent, and Varney.

The progenitor of the Hatfield family of Kentucky and West Virginia was Ephraim, who appeared in Russell County, Virginia, about 1774. He and his second wife, Anne Musick, lived to advanced years, and at their deaths in 1855 they were buried on Blackberry Creek in Pike County, Kentucky, where they had made their home. Valentine, a son of Ephraim, married Martha Weddington and settled on Horse Pen Creek in present Mingo County, West Virginia, where he founded the West Virginia branch of the Hatfield family. His brother Joseph, who resided in Kentucky, established the Kentucky branch.

The immediate ancestor of the principal feudists of the Hatfield family was another Ephraim, the son of Valentine. Over seven feet tall and weighing more than three hundred pounds, he was generally referred to as "Big Eaf." When he was about sixteen years old, "Big Eaf" married Nancy Vance, a sister of Zebulon Vance, the Civil War governor of North Carolina. "Big Eaf" and Nancy made their home on Mate Creek, a West Virginia tributary of the Tug Fork. Ten of their eighteen children lived to maturity, including six sons, Valentine, William Anderson, Elias, Ellison, Smith, and Patterson.

William Anderson Hatfield, the recognized leader of the clan in its feud with the McCoys, was born September 9, 1839. Throughout his life he used the second of his given names, or the nickname of Anse, from which later derived the appellation of "Devil Anse." Shortly after the outbreak of the Civil War he married Levicy Chafin, and they eventually established their home at the mouth of Peter Creek, at the present town of Delorme, West Virginia. They became the parents of thirteen children, including Johnson, or Johnse, William Anderson, Jr., or Cap, Robert E. Lee, Elliott, Elias, Detroit, or Troy, Joseph, Emanuel Willis Wilson, Nancy B., Mary, Elizabeth, Rosada, and Tennyson, or Tennis.[2]

The forefather of the McCoy family, William, lived for a

time, according to family tradition, in Maryland on the site of the battlefield at Antietam. Later McCoy resided in Montgomery County, Virginia, and in 1804 he and his family settled on Johns Creek, in Kentucky, at present Gulnare. His son Daniel married Margaret Taylor in Floyd County, Kentucky, probably in the part that in 1821 became Pike County. Among the thirteen children of Daniel and Margaret was Randolph, the leader of the McCoy side of the famous feud. In 1840 Daniel McCoy and his wife moved to Logan County, (West) Virginia, where they lived until their deaths.

Randolph McCoy, usually called Randall or Ran'l, was born October 30, 1825, in Pike County. On December 9, 1849, he married Sarah, better known as Sally, McCoy, his first cousin. For a time the couple resided in Logan County, but they later returned to Pike County. They made their home on Blackberry Fork of Pond Creek, a tributary of Tug Fork, on property that was willed to Sarah by her father in 1855. Randolph and Sarah became the parents of sixteen children, including Josephine, James H., Floyd, Tolbert, Samuel, Lilburn, Alifair, Rose Anna, Calvin, Pharmer, Randolph, Jr., or Bud, William, Trinvilla, Adelaide, Fanny, and an unnamed child.[3]

The Hatfields, more numerous in West Virginia than in Kentucky, probably constituted the largest clan in the Tug Valley. One political rally in the Tug region in the 1880s attracted over three hundred persons who either bore the name of Hatfield or had Hatfield blood in their veins.[4] The McCoys also lived on both sides of the Tug Fork, but most of them resided in Pike County, Kentucky. Both families were extensively related to other residents of the Tug Valley.

In their physical attributes and their attitudes the Hatfields and the McCoys showed striking similarities. The McCoys have been described as "in general tall and lithe and handsome." Possibly of Lowland Scottish stock, but intermarried with the Highland Celtic strain, some of them had a slightly olive complexion and either dark or auburn hair.[5] The Hatfields tended to be large and to possess great physical strength. One contemporary writer described the Hatfields of the late nineteenth century as "a high spirited family, but . . .

4

kind, neighborly, and just to all who treat them justly." He went on, however, to declare that "an enemy . . . might as well kick over a bee-gum in warm weather, and expect to escape the sting of the insect, as to tramp on the toes of one of these spirited, tall sons of the mountains, and not expect to be knocked down."[6] His words applied equally well to the McCoys.

The Hatfield and McCoy families belonged to the southern yeoman class. Devil Anse Hatfield and Randolph McCoy both owned considerable land and livestock.[7] They and their relatives lived chiefly by farming and hunting, and in later years many of the menfolk engaged in logging operations. Like many dwellers in the hills, some members of the two families carried on the agriculturally related business of making whiskey, which they considered a legitimate way of marketing grain crops. They put up a stiff resistance to the law of 1862 which made illicit distilling a federal offense and which appeared to them a gross violation of individual rights and an unwarranted infringement upon the economic prerogatives of self-sustaining citizens. In this respect, their attitudes were precisely those which in 1794 had spurred Pennsylvania farmers to armed resistance of the whiskey tax imposed by the federal government as part of Alexander Hamilton's financial plans.[8]

Casual visitors sometimes had difficulty in reconciling the independent economic circumstances of families of the Tug Valley, such as the Hatfields and the McCoys, with the crudeness of their dwellings. In 1888 T. C. Crawford, a reporter for the *New York World*, visited Devil Anse at his house on Island Creek, a tributary of the Guyandotte River. The clan leader had recently moved there after disposing of five thousand acres of land on the Tug River. The correspondent described Hatfield's residence, which was similar to the one which he had left, as a two-room dwelling, one room of which served as a kitchen and dining area and the other as sleeping quarters. A narrow passageway between the two rooms was lined with beds and the loft provided additional sleeping space. The McCoy dwelling on Blackberry Fork was also a double log house, with the two parts connected by a roofed passageway. The main part of the house, commonly called the big house, was a story and a half high, and the other, used as a kitchen and bedroom, was but one story.[9]

The isolation of the Tug Valley fostered a prolongation of frontier conditions in which education and organized religion suffered. In 1881 Logan County, which included present Mingo County, had seventy-eight schoolhouses, mostly one-room log structures, but as late as 1890 only 44 percent of the children of school age were enrolled in a primary school. A mere 24 percent of those enumerated were in average daily attendance.[10] In an effort to provide an opportunity for learning, the Hatfields built a small log schoolhouse on Mate Creek. Its teacher, Charles Carpenter, was a staunch Hatfield partisan in their feud with the McCoys. Boasting that he had been shot at at least once a year for seventeen years, Carpenter impressed others more with his penetrating stare and eternal watchfulness than with devotion to learning.[11]

Similar conditions prevailed in Pike County, where the superintendent of schools reported in 1884 that "the greatest part" of the schoolhouses had been condemned under recent legislation and that the best teachers had left the county because of inadequate pay. Most of the Pike County school buildings, like those of Logan County, were constructed of logs.[12] School terms in both counties lasted about three months each year, which was about average for the Appalachian sections of their respective states. Under these circumstances, it is not surprising that the leaders of the Hatfield and McCoy clans and many of their supporters used their marks on legal documents, a forceful reminder of the high rate of illiteracy in the mountains.

The weakness of the common school in Pike and Logan counties was matched by that of another civilizing influence, organized religion. Most of the Hatfields and McCoys appear to have leaned toward the Primitive, or Hardshell, Baptist Church. The Reverend Anderson ("Deacon Anse") Hatfield, a Kentucky cousin of the feud leader of the same name, pastored a church near the junction of Hatfield Branch and

Blackberry Creek in Pike County. At the time of the feud, however, neither of the clan leaders showed much interest in religion. The *New York World* correspondent who visited Devil Anse in 1888 asked his host about his religious views. Devil Anse allegedly replied, "I belong to no Church unless you say that I belong to the one great Church of the world. If you like you can say it is the devil's Church that I belong to."[13] Randolph McCoy, according to a recent chronicler of the McCoy family, believed in God and was certain that no man in his right mind could doubt the existence of the devil, especially if he had lived near the Hatfields.[14]

The weaknesses of the school and the church in the Tug Valley contrasted sharply with the strong bonds that united families. Where the first two languished, family solidarity and loyalty to the clan assumed a special importance in the hearts of isolated mountaineers. The Hatfields and the McCoys exhibited many of the qualities of family life commonly associated with the southern Appalachians. Both families were large, and children were welcome additions. "Seems like a body ought to have at least twelve," a statement attributed to an unidentified mountain woman, might very well have been uttered by Levicy Hatfield or Sarah McCoy.[15] Equally applicable to the feudists was the observation of one writer, "There is always a welcome for the new little son or daughter, while the affection of the older members of the family for the 'least one' is beautiful and touching."[16] At the same time there existed a profound deference to the aged. Hatfields, for example, referred to Sarah McCoy as "Aunt Sally" and to James McCoy, her eldest son, as "Uncle Jim," while the McCoys spoke of Valentine Hatfield, the brother of Devil Anse, as "Uncle Wall."

The upbringing of the mountain boy requires special notice. He often grew up untempered by strong parental or social discipline and with "neither training nor example in self-control." Sometimes his father, in furious temper, whipped him, and at times his exasperated mother carried out an oft-made threat to "wear him out with a hickory," but most of the time he remained free to follow his own impulses. His diversions, such as hunting and fishing, were essentially solitary in nature, and his opportunities for acquiring self-control in social situations were limited.

In many mountain neighborhoods a "gang" spirit differentiated the boys "up the branch," for instance, from those "down the creek." Lacking constructive outlets for expression, this gang spirit often degenerated into a lawless independence and rural insularity manifested in "rocking" individuals and objects that met with disfavor, burning property, robbing orchards, and similar offenses. The mountain youth, sensitive and quick to take umbrage, passionately desired to be the victor in any difference with others. As one observer noted, "Ridicule or the suspicion that someone is 'throwing off on him' he cannot bear, and he is quicker with a knife, or, when he is older, with the pistol, than with his fists."[17]

In their national backgrounds, religious outlook, educational attainments or lack of them, concerns for family unity, and concepts of child rearing, the Hatfields and the McCoys did not differ substantially from other southern Appalachian families. It is futile, therefore, to seek the origins of the feud in characteristics that were as common to families who did not resort to bloodshed as to those who did. The intense family loyalties, generally regarded as contributing to the dimensions of the feud, for example, may have been offset to an extent by connections of the two clans with each other and with other families of the Tug Valley. Although the prevailing characteristics of Tug Valley society may not explain the reasons for the Hatfield-McCoy vendetta, they nevertheless provide an essential backdrop for any understanding of the circumstances which did produce it.

2

THE LEGACY OF
THE CIVIL WAR

Most writers on the Hatfield-McCoy feud, regardless of their conclusions about its origins, agree that it did not begin before the Civil War. Some claim has indeed been made that the vendetta had its beginnings in the English civil strife of the seventeenth century, when the Hatfields allegedly supported Oliver Cromwell and the McCoys defended the rights of the Stuarts and Charles II. If any such division between the two families ever existed, it had totally subsided by the time they settled in Kentucky and West Virginia. For nearly half a century, in fact, they lived at peace with each other in the Tug Valley.

Before the outbreak of violence between their families, Hatfields and McCoys had occasionally intermarried. Two marriages that closely linked them before the end of the Civil War were those of Ephraim Hatfield and Elizabeth McCoy in 1859 and Ellison Hatfield and Sarah Ann Staton in 1865. Ephraim was a cousin of Devil Anse Hatfield, and Elizabeth bore the same relationship to Randolph McCoy. A closer connection between the two families appeared in the marriage of Ellison Hatfield, the brother of Devil Anse, and Sarah Ann Staton, a first cousin once removed of Randolph.[1] Both the Hatfields and the McCoys had intermarried with other prominent families of the Tug Valley, including the Whitts, Weddingtons, Scotts, Blackburns, Justices, Clines, Staffords, Blankenships, Charleses, and Chafins. Many residents of Logan and Pike counties had relatives in both camps during the feud.

Despite the close relationships among the families living there, the Tug Valley experienced the same depth of division and bitterness commonly found in the border states in the Civil War period. The Hatfields favored the Confederacy, as did the majority of the McCoys, but a few of the latter supported the Union. The oft-repeated assertion that the immediate families of Devil Anse Hatfield and Randolph McCoy fought on opposite sides in the war and emerged from the conflict with enduring enmity has no foundation in fact.

About a week after he married Levicy Chafin, Anderson Hatfield joined a local militia company. Although some accounts state that in 1862 he enlisted as a first lieutenant in Company A, Forty-fifth Battalion, Virginia Infantry, and rose to the rank of captain, extant records show that he served as a private in Company D and took unofficial leave on February 1, 1863. In late August of that year, however, he was a first lieutenant in Company B, which was then stationed at Saltville, Virginia.[2]

Devil Anse apparently deserted the Confederate service before the end of 1863. One explanation offered for his departure is that he refused to carry out an order of a court-martial to execute two soldiers, his cousin George Hatfield and Philip Lambert, for taking unofficial leave. Another version is that he lost interest in the Confederate cause after the death of his friend Brigadier General John B. Floyd, who was removed from his command by President Jefferson Davis following the Union capture of Fort Donelson. Floyd later became a major general in the Virginia forces and served in the Big Sandy Valley, where he suffered an extreme exposure that may have contributed to his death on August 26, 1863. Either reason appears to be in keeping with the temperament and character of Devil Anse.

The desertion of Devil Anse, nevertheless, may also be viewed in a broader context. The entry of West Virginia into the Union on June 20, 1863, left Confederate sympathizers within its borders in a precarious position. They had much to lose, both in political rights and property confiscations, by open opposition to the new state in which they resided. By the latter part of 1863 Union forces clearly had the upper hand in most of West Virginia and in eastern Kentucky as well. Moreover, the tide of war had turned against the Confederacy on nearly every major battlefront. Recognizing that their families and property at home were in grave jeopardy and having no desire to become martyrs to a lost cause, numerous Hatfields and McCoys, as well as members of other Tug Valley clans, began to desert the Confederate ranks in the autumn and winter of 1863. The Hatfield deserters included not only Devil Anse but also two of his brothers, Ellison, a second lieutenant, and Elias, a private, and his cousin Ephraim in Company B of the Forty-fifth Battalion. Among the McCoys who left Confederate service was Selkirk, who resided in Logan County. Randolph McCoy also apparently took unofficial leave in 1863, although some accounts maintain that he spent the last years of the conflict as a prisoner of war.[3]

Upon leaving Confederate service, Devil Anse formed a militia unit of Home Guards known as the Logan Wildcats, which operated in Logan, Wayne, Cabell, and other border counties of West Virginia. He and his men may also have ventured into Kentucky. A quarter of a century later, in an interview with a reporter for the *Wheeling Intelligencer*, Devil Anse named three McCoys who had served in his company. According to some accounts, which appear reliable, Randolph McCoy himself was for a time a member of the organization. The loyalties of these men appear to have been flexible, and there is no reason to believe that their activities differed from those of similar guerrilla bands in the Appalachian Mountains.[4]

Both Hatfields and McCoys engaged in irregular military activities, either in the name of the Home Guards or the Confederate Army, which left a legacy of bitterness and resentment between members of the two families. In 1863 Ellison Hatfield, Henry Davis, Moses Chafin, and probably one other

11

person met Asa Peter McCoy and his brother John in the woods near McCoy's home on Brushy Creek, in Pike County, and an exchange of gunfire occurred. Later Hatfield and his companions drove off four of McCoy's hogs, weighing about two hundred pounds each. According to Davis and Chafin, they took the hogs to the home of John Murphy on Mate Creek, in Logan County, where they divided them. In 1872, nine years later, McCoy still had an unsettled suit against those who had taken his hogs.[5] Significantly, Asa Peter McCoy was the brother of Randolph, and Ellison Hatfield was the brother of Devil Anse.

A similar suit involved a charge by Basil Hatfield, a first cousin once removed of Devil Anse, against nine men, among whom were Moses Chafin, Joseph Smith, John Murphy, John Gooslin, and Andrew McCoy, the last possibly a brother of Randolph McCoy. Hatfield charged the party with taking "six head of fat hogs" from him by force in January 1863. Gooslin contended that they had paid Hatfield for the hogs, which they allegedly acquired for Confederate military forces. Some of the defendants, however, settled their differences with Hatfield by compromise. Others were found not guilty.[6]

In 1864 Daniel McCoy and seven other men allegedly seized at gunpoint eight sides of leather belonging to Thomas Hatfield, scattered tan ooze throughout Hatfield's home, and destroyed one of his bee gums. In his defense McCoy declared that he and the others were regular Confederate soldiers under the command of Captain Melville Lawson of the Tenth Kentucky Confederate Cavalry and that they had been detached under Lieutenant Joseph Smith, one of those charged with taking hogs belonging to Basil Hatfield, to obtain the leather. Hatfield, who took his case to court in 1866, remained dissatisfied.[7] Pleasant McCoy, a brother of Randolph, was accused by James H. Lesley of stealing three horses in 1863, but McCoy denied that he had ever taken "a horse beast of any description" from Lesley or anyone else.[8]

Other litigation of a similar nature sprinkles the pages of the Pike County Circuit Court records in the 1860s and 1870s. It leaves no doubt that both Hatfields and McCoys sought personal advantage from disturbed conditions in the Tug Valley and that the Civil War left a residue of ill will that provided a climate conducive to trouble, particularly at times when members of the two families were under the influence of alcohol.

By far the most serious Civil War incident involving the Hatfields and McCoys resulted in the death of Harmon McCoy on January 7, 1865. Harmon, a younger brother of Randolph, waited nearly two years after the war began before he chose sides. He remained at home and tended his farm, cut timber, and rafted logs down the Tug Fork and the Big Sandy. By 1863, however, Union armies had cleared most of Kentucky of Confederate forces, and much of the remaining fighting took the form of guerrilla warfare. Shortly after the birth of his fifth child, Harmon broke with most of his own family and went to Ashland, where he joined Company E of the Forty-fifth Regiment of Kentucky Infantry Volunteers of the United States Army. He enlisted as a private for twelve months. Harmon's military record is spotty, but he spent some time in a Lexington hospital with a broken leg. On December 24, 1864, he was mustered out of service at Catlettsburg.

About the end of December Harmon returned to his home on Peter Creek, but his former friends and neighbors did not extend him a cordial welcome. According to one account, James Vance, an uncle of Devil Anse Hatfield, met Harmon and promised him that the Logan Wildcats would soon pay him a visit. A few days later someone fired at him from ambush as he drew water from his well. Knowing that to remain at home would mean almost certain death, Harmon hid out in a nearby cave. His black slave, Pete, carried him provisions. The guerrillas, most of them apparently West Virginians, traced Pete through the snow to the cave. There they found Harmon, lame and suffering from lung troubles, and killed him.

When Harmon McCoy's body was found, the blame for his death almost naturally fell upon Devil Anse and the Logan Wildcats. Some associates of Devil Anse, however, maintained that at the time of Harmon's death their leader was confined to his bed with a high fever. More likely the real culprit was Jim Vance, a close associate of Devil Anse, who lived on Thacker Creek about four or five miles from Harmon's home. The tall, heavy-set, dark-bearded Vance, himself a later casualty in the feud between the Hatfields and the McCoys, had a reputation, even among his rough associates, for ruthlessness and vindictiveness.

No one was ever brought to trial for the murder of Harmon McCoy. Most of the residents of the Tug Valley probably felt little sympathy for their Unionist neighbor, and even members of the victim's family may have reasoned that he brought his fate upon himself. Harmon's death and the suspicions that fell upon Devil Anse and Jim Vance added a new chill to relations between the Hatfields and the McCoys, which suffered already from the animosities and injuries incident to the Home Guard and guerrilla activities during the last years of the Civil War.[9]

The persistence of grievances deriving from the war does much to explain why a seemingly minor dispute over a hog could produce such enmity between the Hatfields and the McCoys that many writers have considered it the cause of the feud. Mountain families customarily allowed their hogs to run at large in the woods and feed on the mast of beechnuts and acorns that abounded there. Each owner identified his hogs, which were of the long, lean, sharp-nosed variety known locally as razorbacks, by marking their ears with slits, clips, or bits that clearly distinguished them from those belonging to his neighbors.

In the autumn of 1878 Floyd Hatfield, a cousin of Devil Anse, went into the hills, rounded up his hogs, and drove them into pens for fattening at his home near Stringtown, on the Kentucky side of the Tug Fork. Not long afterward, Randolph McCoy, who lived a mile or two away on Blackberry Fork, stopped to exchange a few remarks with Hatfield near the latter's pigpen, when he chanced to see a hog which he said bore the McCoy markings. The hot-tempered McCoy immediately accused Floyd Hatfield, who some writers have erroneously stated was Randolph's brother-in-law, of penning up one of his hogs. Floyd vehemently denied stealing a hog, a charge always taken seriously in the mountains.

Unwilling to forget the matter, Randolph went immediately to the Reverend Anderson Hatfield, a local justice of the peace, who lived a few miles away in Raccoon Hollow. There he brought suit against Floyd Hatfield for recovery of the hog. On the day of the trial, as G. Elliott Hatfield has stated, "the mountaineers deserted their corn fields, moonshine stills, and logging projects to witness the administration of justice at Deacon Hatfield's cabin." Hatfields and McCoys, along with relatives on both sides, arrived in considerable numbers. Members of the two clans, well armed with rifles and revolvers, were more interested in seeing their kinsmen vindicated than in observing the workings of justice.

Deacon Hatfield's situation was fraught with danger. Any decision that he might render was certain to leave one side deeply aggrieved. He therefore resorted to the use of a jury consisting of six Hatfields and six McCoys, hardly the most promising procedure, considering the cold relations between the two families. Among the witnesses called was William Staton, a nephew of Randolph McCoy. Staton's sister Sarah had married Ellison Hatfield, a younger brother of Devil Anse. Staton, who lived on Mate Creek not far from the leader of the Hatfield clan, swore that he had seen Floyd Hatfield mark the ear of the hog with his own brand. His testimony produced a wave of audible indignation among the McCoys, but the stern manner of Deacon Hatfield and the expectation that the McCoy faction of the jury would stand by Randolph combined to prevent more than angry mutterings.

The McCoys and their partisans were totally unprepared for the verdict of the jury, which cleared Floyd Hatfield of the charge against him. To their astonishment, Selkirk McCoy, a cousin of Randolph, declared that he could find no evidence to contradict the testimony of Bill Staton and voted for acquittal of the defendant. From that time on, the McCoys considered Selkirk, whom they had counted on to be a safe juror, an enemy and a traitor to the family. During the months and years that followed, Selkirk, knowing that there was no neutral

15

ground in the trouble between the two families, identified himself completely with the Hatfields.[10]

The unwillingness of the McCoys to accept the decision of the court illustrates one of the problems in establishing a reign of law in the mountains. Judges, justices of the peace, and jurymen, as well as sheriffs, their deputies, and constables, were often so closely related to the litigants that legal decisions were seldom accepted as impartial and final. For the litigious McCoys, legal machinery was but a vehicle for attaining their purposes. They, like the Hatfields and other mountain families, had little real appreciation for the majesty of the law or faith in its just execution. Consequently, when legal decisions did not satisfy them, they resorted to the law that might makes right, a concept that had received powerful reinforcement during the Civil War, when Home Guards and vigilante groups provided much of the law of the hills.

For Bill Staton the infuriated McCoys had no forgiveness. In the months following the trial, Staton, sensing that discretion was indeed the better part of valor, kept to the West Virginia side of the Tug Fork. Yet, he was involved in two or three incidents that arose from the seething hatred against him. The first occurred when he and his brother John, who were laboriously poling a pushboat up the Tug Fork, rounded a bend in the river and suddenly came upon a boat headed downstream and manned by Floyd and Calvin McCoy, sons of Randolph. Both parties immediately poled their crafts to shore and from opposite sides of the river opened fire upon each other. Fortunately, darkness fell before anyone was killed.

Another incident allegedly took place when Sam McCoy, a nephew of Randolph, encountered Staton and Ellison Hatfield tracking a deer on Mate Creek. Sam shot Staton's gun out of his hand and then rushed at him with the intention of killing him. Ellison quickly jumped between the two men and prevented Staton, as well as Sam, from firing. Ellison told them that the trial over the hog had been fair and advised them to forget the matter. Sam left, vowing that he would yet get Staton.

Bill Staton did not take Sam McCoy's threat lightly. One

day, while he was hunting about a mile from the Hatfield Tunnel of the Norfolk and Western Railway, between the present towns of Williamson and Matewan, West Virginia, Staton spied Sam McCoy and his brother Paris. Staton was certain that the McCoys had not seen him and hoped to make the most of his advantage. Accounts of what happened next, however, are so contradictory that none can be accepted as unquestionably correct. According to one version, Staton fired at the McCoys and hit Paris, who collapsed to the ground with a shattered hip. Sam then shot Staton and inflicted a mortal wound. Taking no chances that his enemy might fire again, Sam jumped upon the wounded Staton, who had either dropped his gun or had it forced from him, and shot his adversary again. Another account has Staton leaping upon Paris and sinking his teeth into Paris's jugular vein, whereupon Sam, observing his brother in mortal peril, killed Staton. For good measure, the latter account adds that the hold of Staton upon Paris was so strong that Staton's jaws had to be pried loose after he died.

The McCoy brothers left Staton in the woods. When his body was discovered, the finger of suspicion pointed toward Sam and Paris, who, according to some versions of the story, hid in a cave. Ellison Hatfield, it is said, swore out a warrant for their arrest and asked Devil Anse to serve it, but the latter allegedly refused on the ground that he and the McCoys had been on good terms during the preceding months.

In due course Sam McCoy stood trial for the murder of Bill Staton. He was arraigned in Logan County before Justice of the Peace Valentine, or Wall, Hatfield, a brother of Devil Anse, and a Hatfield-picked jury. Sam's acquittal, on the basis of self-defense, came as a great surprise to the McCoys, but any satisfaction they may have taken in the workings of legal machinery in Logan County was more than offset by their anger that West Virginia authorities had brought Sam to trial at all. Nor did the possibility that Devil Anse himself may have given the word to his brother and the jurors to refrain from any vindictiveness, as some writers have suggested, ameliorate the hostility felt by the McCoys.[11]

17

The trouble over the hog and the killing of Bill Staton added fuel to the fires of hatred that blazed between the Hatfields and the McCoys. Yet, neither marked a clear beginning of the feud, which seems to have had no single point of origin but to have developed from an accumulation of honest grievances and imagined wrongs. The two incidents, like the Home Guard and vigilante activity during the Civil War and the killing of Harmon McCoy, contributed to the tense relations that exploded in the bloody and dramatic events of the 1880s and made the names of Hatfield and McCoy familiar throughout America.

3

ELECTION DAYS ON
BLACKBERRY CREEK

I N THE MONTHS following the death of Staton the Hatfields continued to make frequent journeys into Kentucky, but they always traveled in well-armed bands. One reason for their caution lay in the numerous legal charges against them in Pike County. They included complaints against Devil Anse and Johnse for carrying concealed and deadly weapons, against Floyd Hatfield for giving spirituous liquors to a minor, and against Devil Anse and his brother Elias, as well as Thomas Chafin, Moses Chafin, John Staton, the brother of Bill, Elias Hatfield, Jr., Floyd Hatfield, and Frank Elam, for banding together for the purpose of annoying and disturbing other persons and committing a felonious act. Pike County officials, however, feared to serve warrants against the Hatfields and their friends, who violated Kentucky law with impunity and had no intention of formally answering any of the charges.[1]

The display of armed might by the Hatfields did not prove a sufficient deterrent to further conflict between them and the McCoys. The spring election of 1880 in Pike County brought a new source of trouble. The polls for the Blackberry Creek precinct, where most of the McCoys voted, opened at the house of Jeremiah, or Jerry, Hatfield, which was centrally located at the confluence of Hatfield Branch and Blackberry Creek. The women of the precinct brought an assortment of homemade foods, which they served at convenient locations beneath the fine shade trees that surrounded Jerry Hatfield's house. The men, particularly the candidates, provided more than ample supplies of whiskey for the voters, most of whom cast their ballots early and then remained with their families throughout the day to take advantage of the food and drink and the social opportunities.

The West Virginia Hatfields customarily attended the local elections in Pike County, since they were related to many of the candidates and, like the Kentuckians, enjoyed the social atmosphere. About midmorning a Hatfield party, including Devil Anse and his sons Johnse and Cap arrived at the Blackberry Creek polling place. Their presence transformed what might have been merely a day of raucous inebriation into another tragic event in the lives of the Hatfields and the McCoys.[2]

Johnse Hatfield endeavored to add a bit of romance to the potentially dangerous mixture of politics and liquor that characterized elections on Blackberry Creek. G. Elliott Hatfield described Johnse as "a small-boned rounder of eighteen, on this occasion . . . dressed fit to kill—yellow shoes, new mail order suit, and a high celluloid collar. He was ruddy faced, ham-handed, and sandy haired, with a pair of insinuating blue eyes that set the mountain belles' hearts all a-flutter. He was a great fellow for putting on the dog."[3] Johnse's way with the girls in every way matched his talents for making and selling moonshine, which he carried on with a flagrant disregard for anti-liquor laws.

Not long after the arrival of the Hatfields, a horse approached the polling place, bearing Tolbert McCoy, the twenty-seven-year-old son of Randolph, and, riding behind him, his twenty-year-old sister Rose Anna. Although Johnse had already met Rose Anna, he now found the dark-haired, dark-eyed girl, regarded as one of the most beautiful in the mountains of Pike County, entirely captivating. In the gala atmosphere of the election, he conversed with her in a way that gave no indication of the deep animosities between their families.

Exactly what happened in the ensuing hours is not known precisely, although some writers have described events with an assurance born of their own invention. Apparently, in the afternoon, while many of the men traded stories and yarns or slept off the effects of alcohol and overeating and the women exchanged gossip, Johnse, his judgment already clouded by drink, and Rose Anna, who felt a singular attraction for him, wandered off to a secluded spot. When they returned about dusk, most of the people had left. Rose Anna evidently expressed great fear of returning home and facing the wrath of her father, and Johnse persuaded her to accompany him to the Hatfield residence on Mate Creek. Probably traveling by way of Peter Branch of Blackberry Creek and along Poundmill Run, they at last reached the narrow valley of the Tug. They passed a cliff of coal or slate, on the top of which grew a large chestnut tree, dying, so some said, because of the large number of buzzards that had roosted there in order to eat the dead Yankees that Devil Anse had killed. Finally, they crossed the log bridge that spanned the small stream in front of the Hatfield house.

Once the Hatfields overcame their surprise, they welcomed Rose Anna with their customary hospitality. Most accounts state, however, that Devil Anse raised strenuous objections when Johnse announced his desire to marry Rose Anna. Johnse evidently did not press the matter, perhaps because he had interests in other girls, including Mary Stafford and Nancy McCoy, both cousins of Rose Anna.

Randolph McCoy apparently endeavored to persuade his errant daughter to return home. According to most accounts, he sent three of her sisters, Alifair, Josephine, and Adelaide, to plead with her, but one writer names John Hatfield, a law officer related to both the Hatfields and the McCoys, as his messenger. Rose Anna waited several months before leaving the Hatfields. By then she had become convinced that Johnse would never marry her or cease his pursuit of other women. Most writers have stated that Rose Anna went at once to the home of her aunt, Betty Blankenship McCoy, at Stringtown, or present Burnwell, Kentucky. Betty McCoy was the widow of Allen, the brother of Sarah McCoy, and herself the mother of eleven children. She received the unfortunate Rose Anna with kindness and affection.[4]

Johnse did not leave Rose Anna in peace. When he learned that she was with her Aunt Betty, he began to visit her. The McCoys heard of the visits and determined to put a stop to them. One October evening Johnse and Rose Anna met by prior arrangement at their rendezvous near Tom Stafford's farm between Stringtown and Matewan. They were taken by surprise when suddenly several members of Rose Anna's family, including Randolph and her brothers James, or Jim, Tolbert, and Pharmer, emerged from the bushes. Jim, an officer of the law, told Johnse that the McCoys intended to take him to Pikeville and turn him over to authorities to answer the many indictments against him, from carrying a concealed weapon to selling moonshine whiskey.

Convinced that her family intended to kill Johnse, Rose Anna hastened to the farm of Tom Stafford, where she borrowed a horse, and sped off for Mate Creek to warn the Hatfields. At the cabin of Elias Hatfield, the brother of Devil Anse, she found the clan leader himself. Upon hearing Rose Anna's story, Devil Anse quickly gathered several men, including his son Cap, his brothers Ellison and Elias, Jim Vance, Tom Chambers, and Moses Christian, to go to the relief of Johnse.

Making use of shortcuts, the Hatfields overtook the McCoys and their captive with little difficulty. They surprised the outnumbered McCoys and released Johnse without firing a shot. According to some accounts, Devil Anse intended to shoot Jim McCoy, who had arrested Johnse, but Elias and Johnse himself dissuaded him from violence. Descriptions of the rescue, like other events of the feud, vary so greatly that there is no way of determining exactly what happened. One version of the story maintains that after Devil Anse rescued Johnse, he commanded the McCoys to kneel down and pray. All allegedly obeyed except Jim, who remained standing and dared the leader of the Hatfield clan to shoot. Forced to respect Jim's courage, Devil Anse refrained from using his gun.[5]

By the time of the capture and rescue of Johnse, Rose Anna may have been expecting a child, a circumstance that undoubtedly would have contributed to the unforgiving attitude of her father. Whether a child was actually born, however, remains uncertain. A McCoy tradition maintains that Rose Anna gave birth to a daughter, Sarah Elizabeth, who lived for about eight months and at her death was buried in the McCoy Cemetery near Stringtown. Cap Hatfield, interviewed in 1929, also stated that Rose Anna had a daughter. G. Elliott Hatfield, however, seems to accept a statement attributed to the *Louisville Courier-Journal* that Rose Anna's child was a boy named Melvin, who was still living on January 1, 1888. Yet another tradition is that Rose Anna contracted measles and had a miscarriage.[6]

Rose Anna's later years were not happy ones. Although the Hatfields, including Devil Anse, held her in new respect for her part in warning them of Johnse's capture by the McCoys, she was never to be a Hatfield. Johnse was a man of wandering ways, and after his narrow escape at the hands of Rose Anna's father and brothers, he abandoned her. Nor did Rose Anna's family show a forgiving spirit. Randolph McCoy, in particular, regarded her message to the Hatfields as an unpardonable sin. The troubled relations between Johnse and Rose Anna ended on May 14, 1881, when Johnse married her cousin Nancy, the daughter of Harmon McCoy, who had been killed in 1865, the year of Nancy's birth.

Dramatic as was the romance of Johnse and Rose Anna, it did not cause the feud between the Hatfields and the McCoys. By the time that Johnse took Rose Anna home to Mate Creek the two families had grown accustomed to periodic outbursts of trouble, which eventually subsided. Moreover, the battle lines were never as distinct between them as some writers have maintained. When the McCoys killed Bill Staton, they ended the life of a man who was really more McCoy than Hatfield. Jeff McCoy, Nancy's brother, visited the Hatfields on Mate Creek and received a warm welcome, and the Hatfields continued their ventures into Pike County, although Johnse, in obedience to the wishes of Devil Anse, discreetly remained in Logan County and did not exacerbate the wounds of the McCoys.

Considering the trouble that grew out of the election of 1880, the Hatfields might very well have given serious thought to the danger of attending another one on Blackberry Creek. Such, however, was not their way. When the polls opened at the Blackberry Creek precinct on Monday, August 7, 1882, at the home of Jerry Hatfield, the West Virginia Hatfields appeared, as was their custom. Among them were Elias and Ellison, brothers of Devil Anse. Also present was another Elias, "Bad Lias," the brother of Deacon Anderson Hatfield. "Bad Lias," a hard drinker and a contentious man, lived about two miles up Blackberry Creek. Early in the day, after the whiskey had begun to flow, Tolbert McCoy, the son of Randolph, accused "Bad Lias" of owing a small sum of money, about $1.75, for a fiddle, but Hatfield angrily protested that he had paid Tolbert about three years previously.

With a fight in the making, Tolbert's younger brothers, nineteen-year-old Pharmer and fifteen-year-old Randolph, Jr., backed up his accusation. Deacon Anse, however, broke up the argument. As the day wore on, trouble flared anew, but the constable, Matthew Hatfield, was able to reduce the weapons from guns to fists. At that juncture Ellison Hatfield roused from a drunken slumber and made remarks to Tolbert which led him to turn his wrath upon Ellison. He attacked Ellison with a knife and slashed away at his stomach. Ellison tried unsuccessfully to take the knife away from Tolbert, but the two younger McCoys rushed to the aid of their brother and began cutting away at Ellison. When Deacon Anse again tried to separate the antagonists, Ellison grabbed a rock. At that instant Pharmer resorted to his pistol and shot Ellison in the back. Elias, the brother of Ellison, although still under the influence of liquor, forced the revolver from Pharmer's hand and tried to shoot him. The McCoys at that point ran and sought cover in the nearby woods.

Pursuers quickly overtook the fleeing McCoy brothers and put them in the custody of Justices of the Peace Joseph and Tolbert Hatfield and Constable Matthew Hatfield. Preferring

24

the mercy of the law to the wrath of the Hatfields, the McCoy brothers offered no resistance when the constable placed them under arrest. Observing twenty-six deep gashes among Ellison's wounds, in addition to the bullet hole, and anticipating quick revenge by the Hatfields, Deacon Anse urged that the McCoys be moved to the Pikeville jail immediately. Randolph McCoy reminded the minister, however, that the McCoys were also fighters.[7]

Meanwhile, some of the men made a crude stretcher and carried Ellison across the Tug Fork to the home of Anderson Ferrell, in Warm Hollow, just below the mouth of Blackberry Creek. Believing Ellison to be dying, they sent word to his family. Upon receipt of the news, Valentine, or Wall, Hatfield, the brother of Ellison, sprang to action. He rounded up three Mahon brothers, Dock and Plyant, his sons-in-law, and Sam, all nephews by marriage of Ellison, and the next morning about daybreak they set out for Kentucky. Proceeding by way of Poundmill Run and Blackberry Creek, they very soon encountered Elias, who informed them that Ellison had been taken across the river to Logan County and that the McCoys were under arrest. Wall and Elias agreed to continue on alone and sent the Mahons home.

The guard escorting the McCoys to Pikeville, contrary to the advice of Deacon Anse, had taken the prisoners to Floyd Hatfield's for food and spent the night at the house of John Hatfield, farther up Blackberry Creek. The party left for Pikeville about eight o'clock on the morning of August 8. It had gone only about a mile when Wall and Elias overtook it. Wall, himself a justice of the peace, insisted, in tones of reason and restraint, that the McCoys be tried in the district in which the crime had occurred. He also expressed a desire to obtain relevant testimony from his aged uncle, Valentine Hatfield, and Dr. Jim Rutherford. After some consideration the Kentucky authorities agreed to Wall's request.

Before the men resumed their journey, Devil Anse and a large party of Hatfield supporters arrived, all fully armed. After visiting Ellison at Warm Hollow, Devil Anse and his men had spent the night in an abandoned house near the mouth of Blackberry Creek. The next morning they met the Mahon brothers, who joined them, and all continued to Deacon Anse's, where they obtained food. Devil Anse then stepped forward and called upon all friends of the Hatfields to form a line. Those who joined him included Johnse, Cap, Alex Messer, Joe Murphy, the Mahon brothers, Charley Carpenter, Dan and Jeff Whitt, Tom Chambers, and others. Devil Anse announced to the helpless guards that the Hatfields would take charge of the McCoys, who had been placed in a corn sled, a boxlike vehicle on runners. Carpenter then tied the McCoys with a rope, which he had obtained at Jerry Hatfield's.

Clearly the Hatfields had the upper hand. Wall allegedly turned to Randolph McCoy, who had remained with his sons, and threatened that they would die if any attempt were made to bushwhack the Hatfields. Knowing that he could do nothing to aid his sons and having no confidence in Wall's assertion that all that the Hatfields wanted was that the civil law should take its course, Randolph mounted his horse and sped away for Pikeville for help. After the Hatfield party had ridden about a mile, Devil Anse told Jim McCoy, the older brother of the prisoners, to go back and, according to his own admission, considered forcing the Pike County officials to return also.

At the mouth of Blackberry Creek the Hatfields found a skiff. Devil Anse, Wall, Johnse, Carpenter, and Murphy forced the McCoys into it and crossed the Tug to the West Virginia shore. They led the McCoys upstream and, with dusk approaching and rain threatening, conducted them to an unused log schoolhouse on Mate Creek. About dark, in the midst of a drenching rain, a messenger arrived with a report that Ellison's condition had worsened. The Hatfields hung a lantern near the schoolhouse door, posted guards inside the building and in nearby areas, and waited for further developments.

Not long afterward, while Wall was on guard, Sarah McCoy and her daughter-in-law Mary Butcher, the wife of Tolbert, appeared. Recognizing the women, Wall stopped them at the steps of the building. Sarah began a tearful plea for permission to see her sons. Both Wall and Devil Anse had mixed feelings about granting her request, but Devil Anse finally gave the word to allow them to enter, and he and Wall permitted them to spend a considerable time with the prisoners. By ten o'clock Sarah, crying, praying, and pleading, was nearing hysteria. Charley Carpenter, one of the guards stationed among the trees surrounding the schoolhouse, commanded her to cease. About that time someone shouted that Randolph McCoy was across the Tug Fork, organizing a rescue party, a rumor without a shred of truth. The Hatfields thereupon ordered the sobbing women to leave. They disappeared into the darkness, to spend the night at the home of Dr. Jim Rutherford.

The next morning, while Mary still slept, Sarah returned to Mate Creek, but Wall warned her to leave and not come back. Periodic news concerning Ellison left no doubt that he lay near death, and several of the numerous Hatfield clan who visited the schoolhouse to see the prisoners freely predicted that the McCoy brothers themselves had but a short time to live. Ellison ("Cotton Top") Mounts, reputedly the son of Ellison Hatfield, entered the building and made threats against the McCoys, but Wall ordered him out.

On Wednesday, August 9, 1882, Ellison died. Already, Devil Anse, who had visited his dying brother and heard from his own lips an account of the election-day fight which implicated all three of the McCoys, had decided upon a course of action. When news of Ellison's death reached the schoolhouse, a band of Hatfield partisans helped the prisoners to their feet and marched them off to Kentucky. On the way they met Joe Davis, a witness to the death of Ellison, who confirmed that Randolph, Jr., the youngest of the three brothers, had assisted Tolbert and Pharmer in the stabbing of Ellison. At the mouth of Mate Creek they crossed the Tug Fork to the Kentucky side. There, in a small depression, not far from the riverbank, they stopped and bound the McCoys to some pawpaw bushes. Then, within the space of a few seconds, they fired some fifty shots into the brothers.

Jim McCoy, who had already heard of Ellison's death, was sitting on the porch of Asa McCoy's cabin, at the mouth of

Sulphur Creek, during the firing. Hearing the fusillade, he moved to the edge of the porch and obtained a glimpse of the flashes of the last shots. Later that night, Jim, suspecting that the Hatfields had carried out a threat to put an end to his brothers, gathered some of the men of the neighborhood, including Anderson Ferrell and Sam Simpkins, and crossed over to the Kentucky side of the Tug River. With the aid of lanterns, they climbed to the scene of the shooting, near a sinkhole where men had earlier thrown the carcasses of sheep-killing dogs. Swinging from the bushes were the bullet-riddled bodies of Tolbert and Pharmer. Tolbert's hand was clasped over his head, as if to ward off the bullets, one of which had passed through his skull. Young Randolph remained in a kneeling position, with the entire top of his head blown off.[8]

Following the grisly events of August 9, funerals were held on both sides of the Tug Fork. On the afternoon of August 10 friends of the Hatfields carried the coffin of Ellison Hatfield from the home of his brother Elias to a grave prepared nearby. The following day a similar procession left the McCoy house bearing three hastily constructed coffins. It wound its way down the trail a short distance and then ascended a steep path to a burial ground on a cleared mountain shelf, where the bodies of Tolbert, Pharmer, and Randolph, Jr., were lowered into a single grave.[9]

One significant difference marked the two funerals. That of Ellison Hatfield represented a death avenged. The McCoys went to their graves without retribution by either law or family. Almost immediately after the discovery of their bodies, the coroner had held an inquest, but the jury had announced that they had been killed by persons unknown, a report technically true, since no witnesses testified against the Hatfields and their friends and all evidence of guilt was purely circumstantial.[10]

Although he knew that the alleged murderers resided in West Virginia and that there was almost no chance of extradition, Judge George N. Brown of the Pike County Circuit Court determined that the form if not the substance of justice must be satisfied. He charged a grand jury, without a Hatfield or a McCoy as a member, with naming the killers of the McCoys. After ten days of deliberation, the grand jury returned indictments against twenty men. They were Devil Anse Hatfield, his brothers Wall and Elias, his sons Cap and Johnse, Charley Carpenter, Joe Murphy, Dock, Plyant, and Sam Mahon, Selkirk McCoy and his sons Albert and L. D., Tom Chambers, Lark and Andrew Varney, Dan and John Whitt, Alex Messer, and Elijah Mounts.

Four days later, on September 18, 1882, Judge Brown issued bench warrants for Jacob Puckett, Matthew Hatfield, the Reverend Anderson Hatfield, Richard Hatfield, James McCoy, Tolbert McCoy, an uncle of the murder victims, James Francisco, Anderson Ferrell, John C. Francis, Samuel Simpkins, Uriah McCoy, George Sprouse, Floyd Hatfield, Harriet Simpkins, Mont Stafford, Scott Allen, and Sarah McCoy as witnesses for the state.[11]

When the next term of court convened in February 1883, the sheriff reported that he had been unable to arrest any of the twenty men named in the indictments. Beside each name in the court records he wrote, "Not found in this county February 19, 1883," a phrase that meant nothing more than an admission of the unwillingness of the sheriff and his men to confront the Hatfields, who continued to cross the Tug Fork into Kentucky, but always in heavily armed bands. For over five years the Hatfields and their associates escaped arrest. Their open defiance of civil authority in Kentucky further weakened an enfeebled system of justice in Pike County and contributed to a prolongation of the feud.[12]

4

THE SMOLDERING FIRES

THE HATFIELDS and the McCoys showed little inclination to maintain the tempo of action that characterized the week following the election of 1882, which left Ellison Hatfield and Tolbert, Pharmer, and Randolph McCoy, Jr., dead. Some of them may have occasionally fired upon a member or a cabin of the opposing clan. Stories circulated of men who mysteriously disappeared and of hunters who came upon unidentified bones, which they assumed to be of human origin and about which they kept a discreet silence. Such reports, which may have contained an element of truth, must be accepted, however, with considerable reservation, since the disappearance of a protagonist on either side would not have gone unnoticed or, if need be, unavenged.

Although the feud entered one of its quieter periods, both the Hatfields and the McCoys felt the strain of the constant watchfulness. The Hatfields occasionally rode to Pikeville, but they traveled in companies adequate for their protection and were heavily armed. The McCoys also ventured into West Virginia, and they took the same precautions.

The participation of Devil Anse in the killings appears to have reached a climax with the slaying of the sons of Randolph McCoy. After that incident he became less active in confrontations between the two families, although many regarded him as still the archschemer behind most of the deaths that occurred in later years. The ostensible leader of the Hatfield clan from then on appeared more and more to be Cap, the second son of Devil Anse.

Ironically, as Devil Anse's passion for vengeance appeared to subside, that of Randolph McCoy seemed to increase. Yet even McCoy sought redress by legal means. He pinned his hopes on Perry Cline, a Pikeville attorney and the brother of Martha Cline McCoy, the widow of Randolph's brother Harmon. Described as "a tall, rather stoop-shouldered man, with a pale face and full, long, black beard that extends up to a Blaine nose," Cline had an intelligent, gentlemanly bearing. He had grown up near the Tug Fork, but had moved to Pikeville, where he won election to public office on several occasions. In 1873 he was a successful candidate for the Kentucky House of Delegates, and he also served in the state's Democratic convention. In later years he supplemented his income by serving as deputy sheriff and jailer of Pike County.[1]

Through mountain gossip and their own intelligence, the Hatfields learned that Randolph McCoy was planning a trip to Pikeville, evidently to consult with Cline. Randolph combined a morose nature with a tendency to talk about his troubles with all who would listen. The Hatfields therefore gathered rather precise information about his purposes and plans for travel. Despite an apparent preference on the part of Devil Anse to allow feelings to cool, the Hatfields had no intention of permitting Randolph to array the legal authority of Pike County against them. On the day that he was to leave, members of the Hatfield clan took up positions along the trail that he would use. Their plan, however, miscarried. They shot at two men, whom they mistook for Randolph and his son Calvin, from ambush, wounding one and killing the horses of both. Their victims turned out to be nephews of Randolph, John and Henderson Scott, and the McCoys, who left home somewhat later than they had planned, escaped almost certain death.[2]

Although not connected directly with the feud, an incident in the spring of 1883 reinforced the belief that no Hatfield would willingly submit to confinement in a Kentucky jail. On March 5 a police guard removed Montaville Hatfield, who had been charged with murder, from a Wolfe County jail to the Montgomery County jail in Mount Sterling. Sentiment had run so high in Wolfe County that authorities feared that Montaville's friends might try to rescue him or that his enemies might remove him and kill him. Montaville was the son of Elexious Hatfield, a brother of the Reverend Anderson Hatfield, and a cousin of Devil Anse. At least one newspaper reporter, therefore, could not resist the urge to link him with the activities of the West Virginia clan and even with the murder of the three McCoys in 1882.

One morning the wife of the jailer at Mount Sterling observed a rope made of blankets suspended from an upper-story window of the jail, a clear indication of a jailbreak. An investigation disclosed that three of the prisoners, among them Montaville Hatfield, had escaped by tearing loose a cell door, breaking away a stone supporting the grating over the window, and making the rope of blankets. One newspaper speculated that the escapees had planned their strategy well in advance and had obtained assistance from someone on the outside. Another prisoner stated that the trio had told him of their plans and that they were headed for West Virginia to join their friends and to find safety from Kentucky authorities.[3]

Meanwhile, Johnse, the casanova of the Hatfields, began to have his own problems. Drawn to the McCoys as if by some fatal attraction, he had married Nancy, a cousin of Rose Anna, but neither the Hatfields nor the McCoys looked upon this alliance between their families with approval. Although Johnse had a reputation as a domineering man, Nancy soon established her authority over their household, and it became common knowledge that Johnse was henpecked. The McCoys may have gloated over a kind of victory over the Hatfields, but Devil Anse looked upon Johnse's meekness with disgust.

The Hatfields might have endured Nancy's domination of Johnse, but they could not tolerate her disloyalty to the clan. Not long after the marriage of Johnse and Nancy, they became convinced that someone was providing detailed information of their plans and actions to the McCoys. Nancy, they reasoned, must be the link with the enemy. From Nancy, the trail led to the residence of Bill Daniels, on the West Virginia side of the Tug Fork. Daniels was a peaceable man, who gave no offense to his neighbors, but his wife, Mary, was a sister of Nancy and in every way her equal in her ability to control her husband.

Nancy and Mary thrived on gossip, and the events of the feud between the Hatfields and the McCoys fascinated them. They visited each other frequently and exchanged information freely. In time the Hatfields assured themselves that Nancy and Mary were supplying information to the McCoys. Knowing that neither of their husbands was master in his own house, they decided to take matters into their own hands.

One night Cap, acting for the family, and Tom Wallace burst into the Daniels cabin and held the family at gunpoint. One of them backed Daniels and his daughter against the wall and held them, while the other lashed Mary Daniels with a cow's tail. The intruders then changed places, and one held Mary Daniels and her husband at bay, while the other whipped their daughter, also much given to gossip, with the cow's tail. The two men had nothing against Daniels, but when they left they warned the two women to stay at home and mind their own affairs.

Wallace had his own reasons for the attack. The Daniels girl had lived with him for a time as his wife but had left after finding out that he had tricked her into a mock wedding ceremony. Wallace had not been able to persuade her to return and may have sought vengeance for her leaving. The Daniels family had no difficulty in identifying their assailants, who made no attempt whatever at any disguise, and complained far and wide of the indignities that they had suffered.[4]

Not long after the visit of Cap Hatfield and Tom Wallace to the Daniels cabin, Jeff McCoy, the brother of Nancy and Mary, found himself in trouble. In the fall of 1886, while at a dance, he killed Fred Wolford, a Pike County mail carrier. Upon the advice of his older brother, Lark, who lived on Peter Creek, Jeff decided to leave Kentucky rather than face arrest and possible imprisonment. He made West Virginia and the home of his sister Nancy his destination, confident that he could persuade her husband, Johnse, to accord him the welcome which he expected as a brother-in-law.

At the Hatfield residence Jeff heard details of the attack upon his sister and niece by Cap and Tom Wallace. He allowed his desire for revenge to lead him down a tortuous path to his death. Jeff learned that Wallace, for whom he had a special contempt, was working as a hand at the home of Cap. He formulated a plan for capturing Wallace and taking him to the Pikeville jail. Ignoring the risk that he himself might be arrested, he waited for an occasion when Cap was away from home. Then, with Josiah Hurley, a crony willing to do his bidding, he rode over to the Hatfield farm. The two men tied their horses a short distance from the house and stole upon Wallace, who was working in the yard. Suddenly they sprang upon the unsuspecting Wallace, and before he could offer any resistance they had him on the way to Pikeville.

A mountaineer born and bred, Wallace was not without resources in dealing with men of his own kind. As the trio rode toward Pikeville, he watched his chance and suddenly jumped from his horse and ran into the woods. His captors shot at him but inflicted only a flesh wound. Wallace managed to elude them and to reach Cap's house. He barricaded himself inside the sturdy structure, and McCoy and Hurley tried in vain to force their way in. Wallace tried to shoot one or both of his abductors, but he found no opportunity. On the other hand, he himself remained secure against the bullets which McCoy and Hurley rained against the doors and windows in an attempt to force him out. Foiled in their efforts to recapture him, Jeff and Hurley withdrew from the scene.

When Cap returned and heard of the attack, his temper flared. His fury stemmed not only from the damage to his house but also from the danger to which his wife, who was confined to her bed by illness, had been exposed. The next day he and Wallace appeared before a justice of the peace, and Wallace swore out warrants for the arrest of Jeff McCoy and Josiah Hurley. Cap procured for himself an appointment as a special constable for the express purpose of serving the warrants. In his search for retribution, he proposed to arm himself with the authority of the law as well as the usual deadly accoutrements of the Hatfield clan.

Cap arrested McCoy and Hurley with little difficulty and set out with them for Logan. On the way he and Wallace, who accompanied him, stopped at the house of William Ferrell, near Thacker, on Tug Fork. While they were there, Jeff escaped. Cap and Wallace chased him to the Tug Fork. With his captors in close pursuit, Jeff jumped into the stream and swam toward the Kentucky shore. Bullets from the rifles of his pursuers splashed all around him, but he reached the bank on the Kentucky side. Just when success seemed at hand and he reached for a protruding root to pull himself to safety, a bullet struck him, inflicting a fatal wound, and he fell dying back into the water.[5]

Once again Devil Anse attempted to calm a threatened tempest. On December 26, 1886, in response to a letter from Perry Cline, he wrote the Pikeville attorney that the Hatfields were "very sorry" for the trouble that had occurred. Although it had taken place under "aggravated circumstances," he told Cline, "I know and solemnly affirm that if such could have been prevented by me I would have stoped [sic] the Trouble." The Hatfield spokesman gave a brief description of the attack upon Cap's cabin, the capture of Jeff McCoy, and McCoy's dramatic but unsuccessful attempt to escape. Devil Anse expressed the hope that "if thier [sic] is any ambition Relative to this affare [sic] . . . it will be quieted by a fair statement of the case." He sought to reassure Cline by declaring, "I will say to all the relatives of Jeff McCoy that neither one of the Hatfields has any animosity against them" and that he himself was "very sorry that such has occured [sic] and sincerely Trust[ed] that their [sic] will be no more Trouble in regard to the matter."

Devil Anse concluded his letter by saying, "Perry[,] the very Bottom of this crime is nothing more nor less than Mary Daniels and her girls. Now Bill [Daniels] is going and says he wont [sic] come back. No person is going to trouble him; let him come back." The letter, written for Devil Anse by an un-

identified person, has the ring of genuine sincerity. Addressing Cline by his given name and signing himself "Your friend,"
Devil Anse clearly hoped to restore a measure of peace to
relations between the Hatfields and the McCoys.[6]

Unlike Devil Anse, however, some members of both the
Hatfield and McCoy families yearned for revenge. They included Cap Hatfield and Jim Vance on one side and on the
other Randolph McCoy and Asa Harmon McCoy, Jr., known
as Bud, whose father had been killed by the Hatfields and who
himself had a reputation as one of the most dangerous men in
Kentucky. With men such as they thirsting for blood, any efforts at calming the turbulent waters had little chance of
success.

5

AN ERA OF VIOLENCE

THE HOPES OF Devil Anse Hatfield that he might calm the volatile situation following the killing of Jeff McCoy by adopting a conciliatory attitude rested upon the assumption that the clan leaders themselves could control future events. The 1880s, however, brought unusual turbulence to Kentucky, with much of it rooted in Civil War and political discord, with whiskey acting as a catalyst for both. In many respects the Hatfield-McCoy feud was a manifestation of a deep political and social malaise that fostered widespread troubles in eastern Kentucky. Perhaps no clan leader such as Devil Anse could give complete assurances against further eruptions.

Until the late 1880s the vendetta between the Hatfields and the McCoys attracted little attention outside the Tug Valley. Even the murders resulting from the election of August 1882 received no special notice in the newspapers of Kentucky and West Virginia. Election-day violence, with fights, stabbings, and killings, was common in Kentucky and more or less accepted as an unfortunate concomitant of the democratic process. The *Louisville Courier-Journal* of August 8, 1882, in a roundup of election news over the state, reminded its readers that the mixture of politics and whiskey had proved as explosive as ever. Even in Lexington, the hub of the elite Bluegrass society, "King Whiskey held high carnival" and led to considerable fighting in the "ancient streets."

Nor did the trouble between the Hatfields and the McCoys

contrast sharply with conditions prevailing along the Kentucky-West Virginia border. An almost unrestrained lawlessness in parts of the Big Sandy Valley, including Lawrence and Boyd counties, as well as adjacent Carter County, led to the organization of a Regulator movement, which drew the support of some of the leading citizens. The Regulators succeeded in obtaining state troops and then voluntarily disbanded. The *Greenup Independent* declared, with satisfaction, "Inefficient men have been in office, the laws were not enforced and justice went by default, encouraging crime and iniquity, until the people, propelled by natural laws of reaction, put a stop to it."

The newspaper reacted too swiftly. The Regulators had attracted, along with public-spirited citizens, "a band of cutthroats" who engaged in pillage, marauding, and even murder. When an attempt was made to lynch two prisoners confined to the jail in Catlettsburg, Judge George N. Brown directed their removal to Lexington and a change of venue to Carter County. As the prisoners were led onto a steamboat, an Ashland mob aboard a ferryboat fired upon the militia assigned to escort them to Lexington. The troops returned the fire, and the exchange left several persons on the ferryboat and others on the wharves wounded.[1]

Perhaps most residents of the Tug and Big Sandy valleys had greater concern about bands of criminals, which sometimes operated with impunity, than for the Hatfields and the McCoys, who usually molested only each other. The arrest of Steve and Charles Kelley at Ceredo, West Virginia, in March 1888, for instance, exposed a ring that had committed robberies and murders in Kentucky, West Virginia, and Ohio over a period of several months with no real deterrence by authorities in any of the states.[2]

Other bloody vendettas of the eastern Kentucky mountains frequently eclipsed events along the Tug Fork. Breathitt County had a succession of feuds which kept it in a turmoil for a quarter of a century. Probably the first of them began during the Civil War, when John Amis and William Strong raised a company of Unionists in deeply divided territory. After Amis was killed in 1873, the feud "burned itself out," but Strong soon entered into another with Wilson Callahan, which resulted in several deaths before Callahan's assassination ended the trouble. As that vendetta drew to a close, the Jett-Little feud claimed public attention until it put an end to the lives of its principal participants. When Judge John Burnett was killed in 1878, allegedly by members of the Gamble and Little families, Judge William Randall of the criminal court of the district that included Breathitt County declared that he would see the assassins punished. He failed to intimidate the lawless elements, however, and a fight in his own court in which Bob Little was killed and another man was wounded broke up the session and put the judge himself to flight. Randall never returned to Breathitt County to hold court during his remaining tenure as a judge.

Worse disorders lay ahead for Breathitt County. On November 13, 1888, Circuit Court Judge Henry Clay Lilly wrote Governor Simon Bolivar Buckner that he would not attempt to hold court in Breathitt, Letcher, and Knott counties unless the governor provided a state guard, such as some of the previous judges had obtained. Lilly explained that the people were so divided that a sheriff's posse could not maintain order. He declared that several persons charged with murder, including a brother of the sheriff and a son-in-law of the jailer, awaited indictments because witnesses feared to speak out. Jurors were equally cowed, and at the previous term of court four murderers had escaped justice because of hung juries.

Governor Buckner, in a letter of rebuke to Lilly, revealed a strong aversion to state intervention in the Kentucky mountain feuds. He declared that he failed to find, from Lilly's statements or any other source, "an evidence of any organized opposition to the civil authorities" of Breathitt County. The governor reminded Lilly that "in a republic the employment of the military arm in enforcing the law is of rare necessity." He pointed out that "the law invests the civil authorities with ample powers to enforce the observance of the law, and expects those officers to exert their authority with reasonable diligence. When this is done," he wrote, "there is seldom an occasion when the military arm can be employed without bringing the civil authorities into discredit. When a people are taught that they are not themselves the most important factor in the conservation of order in society, and that they must depend upon the exertion of extraneous forces to preserve order among themselves, they have lost their title to self-government, and are fit subjects to a military despotism."

The worst disorder in Breathitt County, known as the Hargis-Cockrell-Marcum-Callahan feud, had its origins in a political contest in which fusion candidates accused County Judge James Hargis and Sheriff Ed Callahan of stealing the election. Violent disputes resulted in warrants for the arrest of Hargis and John B. Marcum, an attorney for the fusionists. Hargis alleged that in arresting him Tom Cockrell, the town marshal of Jackson, and his brother James had drawn a gun on him and would have killed him had not Callahan intervened. Recriminations filled the air during the ensuing weeks, and violence erupted when Cockrell killed Ben Hargis, a brother of the judge, in a blind tiger saloon in Jackson. Cockrell gained strong support from Marcum, who volunteered to defend him, and Dr. D. B. Cox, Jackson's most prominent citizen. Shortly afterward, Jerry Cardwell, also allied with the Marcum, Cockrell, and Cox faction, killed John ("Tige") Hargis, whom subsequent evidence revealed at fault in the altercation.

In the wake of these events Judge Hargis surrounded himself with paid killers. Shortly afterward assassins cut down Dr. Cox, James Cockrell, and Marcum, whose death occurred in front of the courthouse, with Hargis and Callahan watching from a store across the street. For fifteen minutes Marcum lay bleeding before anyone summoned up the courage to attend him. After this reign of terror, state troops arrived. Their presence gave Captain J. B. Ewen, who was with Marcum at the time, the nerve to tell all he knew. On the strength of his testimony, Hargis and Callahan were indicted for murder, but both were acquitted. Hargis, whose near-absolute power in

Breathitt County and gubernatorial connections seemed to give him immunity from punishment in Kentucky, was killed by his own son in 1908, and Callahan was shot from ambush in 1912.[3]

Meanwhile, Hazard, in Perry County, became the center of another feud known as the French-Eversole War. Benjamin Fulton French and Joseph Eversole, the chiefs of their respective clans, were prominent lawyers and successful in the mercantile business. Their trouble began in a business rivalry and a malicious report of a clerk in French's store that French intended to kill Eversole. The two leaders began to gather their forces, made up not only of relatives but also of others to whom they promised employment and good wages. With the killing of Silas Gayhart, a French partisan, in an ambush involving at least a dozen white men and several blacks in the summer of 1887, the town of Hazard became an armed camp. After intermittent fighting, the two sides agreed to lay down their arms, with French surrendering his to the county judge of Leslie County and Eversole placing his in the custody of Josiah Combs, the judge of Perry County, who was his father-in-law.

The armistice proved of short duration. Before long French charged that Eversole was repossessing the weapons that he had deposited with Judge Combs. On September 15, 1887, Eversole and his men waylaid and killed the Reverend Bill Gambriel, a French supporter, who "would fight at the drop of a hat and drop the hat himself." Several members of the Eversole faction were indicted for murder, but only one was tried, and he was eventually acquitted.

After a relatively calm winter, violence flared up again on April 15, 1888, when members of the French forces attempted an ambush of Joseph Eversole, Judge Combs, and Combs's nephew, Nick, as they journeyed to the regular term of the circuit court. The Eversoles, led by John Campbell, thereupon placed patrols in the streets and around the town of Hazard and ordered them to shoot anyone who attempted to enter without a secret password. Sporadic killings, nevertheless, continued.

41

Upon instructions from the governor, Kentucky Adjutant General Sam E. Hill visited Hazard in November 1888. He reported that the population of the town, normally about one hundred, had dwindled to about thirty-five as a result of the tension. Hill found that although he could obtain a fairly accurate account of the killings, he could not say what the feud was all about. He declared, without equivocation, that the failure of authorities to act with promptness and decisiveness at the inception of the troubles had allowed them to get out of hand. Moreover, despite the fact that Eversole and his friends appeared to be the aggressors, the county judge had refused to issue warrants for their arrest, and the two sides sought safety "in arming such persons as would take service with them."

On the basis of his findings, Hill ordered a company of militia to Hazard to protect Judge Lilly's court. As soon as the militia were removed, violence broke out again, and arsonists burned the courthouse. At a special term of court, held in August 1890 in a large tent, Lilly, again supported by troops, stiffened his attitude. As soon as the grand jury made indictments, he ordered the transfer of the prisoners to the Clark County Circuit Court for trial. By removing the trial from the scene of the disorders, the court broke the back of the feud. The only flare-up afterwards came in 1894 with the assassination of Judge Combs.[4]

The troubles between the unschooled Hatfields and McCoys in the mountain recesses of the Tug Valley hardly appeared exceptional when compared with the feuds that raged in the seats of Breathitt and Perry counties between prominent political and business figures. None of them excited the concern at the state level that arose from the Tolliver-Martin-Logan vendetta, which made a shambles of law and order in Rowan County.

The Rowan County troubles had their origin in a political contest in 1874 in which young Thomas F. Hargis, a former Confederate captain and a Democrat, ran against Republican George M. Thomas for judge of the circuit court. Opponents of Hargis charged that he was neither old enough nor had the experience required by law for the position. When Hargis tried to produce proof, he found the entry concerning his admission to the bar cut from the record book at Morehead and data concerning his birth missing from the family Bible. He accused his political enemies of the excisions, and they charged that he himself had removed the evidence. Hargis lost the election by twelve votes in a race which left the county deeply scarred and divided. In 1876, however, he won election to the newly created Circuit Court of Kentucky, and three years later he succeeded Judge J. M. Elliott as a member of the Appellate Court of Kentucky.

Political tensions generated by the 1874 election continued to stimulate election-day troubles. On August 1, 1884, Floyd Tolliver, a resident of Farmers, near Morehead, shot and wounded John Martin, the son of a prosperous Rowan County farmer. A battle ensued in which Solomon Bradley, an innocent bystander, was killed and Adam Sizemore was wounded. Sheriff John C. Day was charged with the shooting of Sizemore. Without delay, the Tolliver, Martin, Sizemore, and Day factions began to line up supporters.

The following December, Floyd Tolliver and John Martin met in a barroom. A fight took place, and Martin killed Tolliver. Fearing that a mob might try to lynch Martin, the county attorney arranged for his transfer to the Clark County jail at Winchester. After unsuccessful efforts to have Martin returned to Morehead, A. M. Bowling, a Tolliver kinsman who served as town marshal of Farmers, and four deputies presented a forged document to the jailer at Winchester and prevailed upon him to release Martin to their custody. A short time earlier Martin's wife had visited her husband and assured him that Rowan County officials would not ask for his return. When the eastbound Chesapeake and Ohio train left Winchester, Bowling had Martin aboard. As soon as the train pulled into Farmers, Craig Tolliver, a brother of Floyd and the recognized head of the Tolliver clan, boarded it with a large party and killed Martin. Only when she heard the commotion did Martin's wife, who returned home on the same train, realize what had happened.

In the weeks that followed, members of the Martin faction

shot from ambush and wounded County Attorney Z. Taylor Young, whom they accused of being pro-Tolliver. Acting in revenge, Tolliver supporters killed Deputy Sheriff Stewart Baumgartner in almost the same spot. In April 1885 the Martins, led by Cook Humphrey, and the Tollivers, led by Craig, took up positions in Morehead and engaged in a battle that raged for hours and left the town and the county in a state of anarchy. Adjutant General John B. Castleman, with state troops, restored order and summoned leaders of the two factions to Louisville, where they agreed to a truce.

The compromise lasted but a few weeks. An unsubstantiated confession by an associate of Humphrey that the family of John Martin had hired him to kill Young and that Humphrey and Baumgartner had arranged details of the plot stirred up trouble again. The Tollivers kept Humphrey and the Martins, who vehemently denied the charges, under close surveillance. In July 1885 they fired into the Martin house near Morehead, killed one of the defenders, and flushed out Humphrey, who miraculously escaped injury although the attackers shot off most of his clothes.[5]

After further troubles, Judge Asher C. Caruth persuaded Humphrey and Craig Tolliver, the recognized leaders in the war, to leave Kentucky permanently. Humphrey, who until his term as sheriff had been outside the feud and widely respected, left and never returned. Tolliver, however, came back to Rowan County, where he gained control of the courts and the grand juries, made Morehead a wide-open town for whiskey, gambling, and other crimes, and instituted a reign of terror. He forced enemies of the Tollivers to leave Morehead, the population of which dropped from seven hundred in 1885 to less than three hundred in 1887, with some of the most respected citizens in the exodus.[6]

Craig Tolliver made a fatal mistake when, at his instigation, a sheriff's posse killed twenty-five-year-old Billy Logan and his eighteen-year-old brother Jack, who lived a few miles from Morehead. The cruel slaughter of the two young men and the burning of their cabin aroused the anger of their cousin, young D. Boone Logan, a quiet, cultured attorney of Rowan

County. Boone Logan himself received a warning from the Tollivers to leave, coupled with an insulting promise that they would provide his wife with employment as a domestic in order that she might support their children.

Logan took the matter to Governor J. Proctor Knott, who explained the constitutional and legal barriers to his rendering any assistance. The young attorney allegedly then told the governor, "I have but one home and but one hearth. From this I have been driven by these outlaws and their friends. They have foully murdered my kinsmen. I have not engaged in any of their difficulties—but now I promise to take a hand and retake my fireside or die in the effort."

Boone Logan succeeded where seemingly stronger men had failed. He purchased Winchester rifles, pistols, and shotguns, with adequate ammunition, and had them shipped under the label of sawmill equipment to Gates station near Morehead. Quietly he then gathered his forces and on June 22, 1887, engaged the Tollivers in open battle in Morehead. At the end of two hours of fighting, Craig Tolliver lay dead, and most of his associates were either killed or wounded. Logan thereupon took control of the town and held it until state troops arrived. The battle was the last bloody clash between the opposing factions in Rowan County. Several of Logan's associates were indicted for murder, but all were acquitted by a Fleming County jury. Logan himself was never tried.[7]

In 1888 an investigating committee of the Kentucky General Assembly visited Morehead. Its report, which traced the origins and development of the feud, declared that between August 1884 and June 22, 1887, twenty murders and assassinations had taken place and sixteen other persons had been wounded in the county. Yet, "during this period there was not a single conviction for murder, manslaughter or wounding, except for the killing of one Hughes, who was not identified with either faction." Moreover, the committee found scores of persons charged with selling liquors without license, carrying concealed deadly weapons, disturbing religious worship, and other breaches of the peace, who had never been arrested or who had posted worthless bonds.

The investigators declared that "county officials were not only wholly inefficient, but most of them [were] in the warmest sympathy with crime and criminals," even going so far "as to rescue criminals from the custody of the law, being totally oblivious to their duty to the commonwealth." They singled out Circuit Court Judge A. E. Cole for censure, for his leanings toward the Tolliver side in the feud, but they admitted that "any Judge in the Commonwealth could not have enforced the law in that county." A proposal for the abolition of Rowan County and attaching parts of it to adjacent counties, however, failed to muster the necessary legislative support.[8]

The legislative investigation confirmed assessments of other observers. Referring to the "epidemic of murder" that had engulfed the county, Attorney General Parker Watkins Hardin in 1885 placed much of the blame upon the grand jury, which was "organized, I know, to shield the strong and guilty and to punish the weak and defenseless" and was itself made up of "criminals, their close kin and steadfast friends and admirers." Reflecting upon the charge by the attorney general, the *Louisville Courier-Journal* observed that it really constituted an admission that "lawlessness has pushed justice aside and taken possession of the machinery of law to protect crime."[9]

In drawing attention to the problems of Judge Cole, the legislative committee investigating affairs in Rowan County touched a critical factor in the maintenance of law and order. Judge William L. Jackson of the Louisville circuit, who agreed to hold court in Breathitt County, demonstrated the importance of a fearless, impartial jurist. Jackson, a member of a prominent West Virginia family noted for its audacity, opened court with a large part of the people of the county on hand, many of them out of curiosity. When witnesses were called in the first case, which involved a murder, all answered except one. Jackson looked the sheriff squarely in the eye and commanded him to produce the missing witness. The sheriff, accustomed to more lax procedures, explained that he could not find the witness. "That's no excuse, sir," replied Jackson.

"Have him here without fail in four hours." He then recessed the court. With that, Jackson left the bench "with dignified ease, calmly put on his hat, and walked from the courtroom alone, to the great astonishment of the natives, whose regular Judge would have remained until perfectly satisfied that no enemy was near."

When the court reconvened at two o'clock, the appointed hour, Jackson asked the sheriff if he had the missing witness. The sheriff stated that when he reached the house of the witness he found it barricaded and full of armed mountaineers, who swore that they would kill any man who attempted to enter. Jackson reprimanded the sheriff, declaring, "Mr. Sheriff, such an excuse is not to be thought of and will not be entertained. I want the witness here at 10 o'clock tomorrow morning if you have to bring him in on a litter. Mark you, sir, a failure to comply on your part will compel the court to fine and imprison you to the full extent of the law. Do your duty, sir."

At ten o'clock the following morning, when the court reconvened, the sheriff produced the witness, carried by half a dozen stalwart men. According to the Louisville correspondent of the *New York Times*, "One arm hung limp at his side, a leg refused to do its duty, blood trickled from all over his head, and an immense bandage concealed one eye." Jackson bade the man to stand up and demanded why he had failed to appear. The witness explained that he had been hiding from federal marshals who planned to take him to Louisville to answer a moonshining charge. Jackson demanded that the marshals be brought before the court and declared to the eight of them who appeared that he would jail them if they attempted any further interference with the court. From then on cases were heard in an orderly manner, with more convictions than in the previous history of the county. Unlike some judges in the "bloody belt" of Kentucky, who refused to hold court without the support of state troops, Jackson acted on the premise that "this court is equal to a hundred men itself."[10]

The Hatfield-McCoy feud, unlike those of Rowan and Breathitt counties, was devoid of any contest for political power. Yet it, no less than the other vendettas of eastern Kentucky, had political overtones in that the Hatfields and the McCoys, in their respective counties, represented a substantial body of voters with which any candidate for office or elected official had to reckon. Although Pike County escaped the bloody political battles that wrecked orderly government in several other counties, it, too, suffered the same weaknesses in the preservation of law and order and the administration of justice. This ineffectiveness provided fertile soil in which the Hatfield-McCoy feud could grow. Had there been an infusion of the spirit of Judge Jackson into the judicial affairs of Pike County, as well as Logan County, West Virginia, the Tug Valley would almost certainly have been spared some of the bloodiest scenes in its history, which loomed on the horizon.

6

INFLAMMATORY POLITICS

Pike County shared both the political and judicial afflictions which prevailed in much of eastern Kentucky. The Hatfield and McCoy clans, like the feuding factions of Breathitt, Perry, Rowan, and other counties, were large and politically significant. They or their partisans frequently held positions of administrative and judicial responsibility, ranging from sheriffs to justices of the peace and constables, and dominated juries, as did the feudists in other counties. When it came to dealing with the Hatfield-McCoy feud, law-enforcement authorities in Pike County proved no more effective than those in other disturbed sections of Kentucky. Nor did the authority of the state, usually asserted with reluctance, gain in strength as it flowed from Frankfort to this easternmost of Kentucky's counties.

The Hatfield-McCoy feud posed special problems for law enforcement in Pike County, for, unlike most mountain vendettas, it transcended not only county lines but also state boundaries. The dominance of the McCoy faction in Pike County and the relative neutrality of the Kentucky branch of the Hatfield family gave the McCoys a clear advantage there. County officials who aspired to use the feud for personal advantage had no choice except to align themselves with the

McCoys. The same situation, in reverse, existed in Logan County, West Virginia, where the Hatfields had a powerful influence.

The gubernatorial race in Kentucky in 1887 demonstrated the close connection between the Hatfield-McCoy feud and Pike County politics. Perry Cline, the ambitious Pikeville lawyer and politician and a brother of the widow of Harmon McCoy, promised to deliver the McCoy votes to Simon Bolivar Buckner, the Democratic candidate. In return, Buckner, who faced an uphill battle, evidently agreed that if he were elected he would use the powers of his office to bring the Hatfields to justice. Cline, a staunch partisan of the McCoys, ignored an earlier appeal of Devil Anse Hatfield for détente. Pressed by Randolph McCoy, who declared that someone, presumably a Hatfield supporter, had recently fired at him from ambush, Cline did much to keep the fires of hostility alive.

The prospects of the use of authority of the state of Kentucky struck the Hatfields not as an intervention in the interest of justice but as the employment of the judicial and military power of the Commonwealth for the benefit of the McCoys. The Hatfields had no intention of submitting their fate to any Kentucky court or of yielding to any extradition procedures. Anticipating efforts to capture them, they organized a vigilante force which they called the Logan County Regulators.

Following the election of Buckner as governor, the Logan County Regulators met at Logan and addressed a letter to Perry Cline, whom they regarded as the principal political agitator against them. Dated August 29, 1887, the letter asserted, "My name is Nat Hatfield. I am not a single individual by a good many, and we do not live on Tug River, but we live all over this county. We have been told by men from your county that you and your men are fixing to invade this county for the purpose of taking the Hatfield boys, and now, sir, we, forty-nine in number at present, do notify you that if you come into this county to take or bother any of the Hatfields, we will follow you to hell or take your hide, and if any of the Hatfields are killed or bothered in any way, we will charge it up to you, and your hide will pay the penalty."

The letter continued, "We are not bothering you and neither are the Hatfields, and as long as you keep your hands off Logan County men, we will not do anything, but if you don't keep your hands off our men, there is not one of you will be left in six months. There is present at this time forty-nine of the men who regulated matters at this place a short time ago and we can get as many as we need in six hours. We have a habit of making one-horse lawyers keep their boots on and we have plenty of good strong rope left, . . . and our hangman tied a knot for you and laid it quietly away until we see what you do. We have no particular pleasure in hanging dogs, but we know you and have counted the miles and marked the tree."[1]

Meanwhile, Jacob and Larkin McCoy, brothers of Nancy, Mary, and Jeff, crossed the Tug Fork with the intention of capturing Cap Hatfield and Tom Wallace and taking them to the Pikeville jail. They never apprehended Cap, but they succeeded in taking Wallace. Caught by surprise, Wallace went along peacefully, but he challenged the right of the McCoys to arrest him without either warrant or extradition papers. Within a week after his confinement, however, Wallace escaped from the Pike County jail under circumstances that suggest some kind of collusion between him and the jailer, whom he had once befriended.

Furious that their prisoner had escaped, Jake and Lark McCoy vowed that they would never return Wallace to the jail at Pikeville. In the spring of 1887 Wallace was found dead in West Virginia. To the suggestion that they killed him, the McCoy brothers only laughed and replied that they had only taken Wallace to jail. Another account of the death of Wallace holds that two bounty hunters, both strangers, approached Jake and Lark and announced that they had come to collect a reward which the McCoys had offered for Wallace. One of the strangers explained that they could not bring Wallace's body from West Virginia but that they had tangible evidence of his death. He then drew from his coat a scalp with a white streak down the center, one of Wallace's most prominent features. Convinced that the scalp was indeed that of Wallace, the McCoys promised the strangers the reward money.[2]

Ignoring both the threat made against him by the Logan County Regulators and the precipitous action of Jake and Lark McCoy, Perry Cline proceeded with his own plans. From the clerk of the Pike County Criminal Court he obtained copies of the indictments against the Hatfields, which in 1884 had been transferred from the Pike County Circuit Court. Cline hoped to use the indictments to induce Governor Buckner to offer a reward for the arrest of the Hatfields and to make a requisition upon the governor of West Virginia for their delivery to Kentucky. On September 6, 1887, accompanied by Lee Ferguson, the Pike County attorney, and Frank Phillips, a deputy sheriff, Cline left for Frankfort.[3]

On September 10 Governor Buckner, pressed by the Pike County delegation, fulfilled his campaign promise to Cline. He made a formal requisition upon Governor Emanuel Willis Wilson of West Virginia for the return to Kentucky of Devil Anse Hatfield and nineteen others charged with the murder of the three sons of Randolph McCoy on the evening of August 9, 1882. In addition, he announced that in accordance with a recommendation of Tobias Wagner, the Pike County judge, the state of Kentucky would offer a reward of five hundred dollars for the apprehension of Devil Anse and his delivery to the jailer of Pike County. Upon the advice of Cline, Buckner named Pike County Deputy Sheriff Frank Phillips to receive the prisoners, provided, of course, the governor of West Virginia chose to honor the request for extradition.[4]

In designating Frank Phillips as his agent, Buckner further enmeshed the Hatfield-McCoy feud in the politics of Pike County and detracted from any possibility of an impartial and disinterested application of the law. Phillips was a man of unquestionable courage, and both Buckner and Cline could trust him to carry out their instructions. Unfortunately, he had a tendency to act impetuously and cruelly, particularly when under the influence of liquor. Kentucky Adjutant General Sam E. Hill described him as "a handsome little fellow, with piercing black eyes, ruddy cheeks, and a pleasant expression, but a mighty unpleasant man to project with." Like Johnse Hatfield, he had a reputation for his amorous pursuits, a trait that lowered him in the esteem of more sedate members of the McCoy family.[5]

On September 30, 1887, three weeks after he made his requisition upon Governor Wilson, Buckner received a reply. Wilson stated that he could not comply with Buckner's requisition since the Kentucky governor had not included an affidavit from the Pike County authorities, as required by West Virginia law. Buckner removed that technical obstacle by sending the required affidavit on October 13. Three more weeks passed, however, without any further word from West Virginia.[6]

Governor Wilson was under considerable pressure to resist any compliance with Buckner's requisition. The Hatfields employed legal counsel, flooded the governor's office with petitions, affidavits, and material designed to convince him of the rightness of their cause and the injustice that they would endure if he delivered them to Frank Phillips. They drew attention to the influence of the McCoys with Pike County officials and contended that they could never receive a fair trial in that county. Moreover, they reminded Wilson that the McCoys had committed various felonies in West Virginia for which they had never been punished.[7]

Suspicious that Wilson's delay in replying to Buckner's second letter was deliberate, Perry Cline on November 5 abandoned all protocol and addressed a letter of his own to the West Virginia governor. He stated that, in accordance with Wilson's request, he had made an "affadavid" and returned it with the "requision" for the West Virginians indicted for the McCoy murders. Since he had heard nothing from Wilson, he asked for information on the status of the matter. Referring to the petitions which the Hatfields had circulated in their own behalf, Cline told Wilson, "They have and can make the people sign any kind of petition they want. I was rased [sic] near them [sic] men and know them; they are the worst band of meroders [sic] ever existed in the mountains, and have been in arms since the war; they will not live as citizens ought to; they stand indicted in the county in 4 bad cases of murder, and one of them which occurred about a year ago, and—last year's court was indicted for Ku-Kluxing and various other misdemeanor cases; in fact, we cannot hold our elections without them crossing the line and rung [sic] our citizens from the election grounds, and selling them liquors in violation of the law, and these men has [sic] made good citizens leave their homes and forsake all they had, and refuse to let any person to even tend their lands."

Cline denied reports, allegedly circulated by the Hatfields, that the Pike County officials wanted them in order to kill them. He declared, "We want peace and want the laws executed, & do not want our citizens butchered up like dogs, as these men is [sic] doing." Professing an interest only in seeing the laws obeyed, he continued, "We believe every person ought to answer for his conduct; that is the reason we ask the requision [sic]." In an effort to establish his own credibility, Cline told Wilson, "You can find out all about myself by writing any of our [Pike County] officers or to any of our state officers, and learn whether or not I am a man of my word."[8]

Without responding to the pleas of the Hatfields, Governor Wilson directed the secretary of state of West Virginia, Henry S. Walker, to inform Cline that he would honor the requisition of Buckner for all the men named in the indictments except Elias Hatfield and Andrew Varney. Walker, who wrote his letter on November 21, explained that the two men had proved to the satisfaction of the governor that they were miles away from the scene of the murder of the three McCoy brothers. Walker informed Cline that he would issue warrants for the others named in the indictments as soon as he received the fees, amounting in all to fifty-four dollars, which the law required.[9]

Tired of waiting, Cline obtained bench warrants from the Pike County Court for the arrest of the twenty men named in the indictments. On December 12, less than a week later, Pike County Sheriff Basil Hatfield had his first arrest. Ironically, the seized man was Selkirk McCoy, for whom the

McCoys had carried a special grudge since his testimony against the claims of Randolph McCoy in the hog trial in 1872. Frank Phillips, Hatfield's deputy, gathered a posse and crossed the Tug Fork to West Virginia, where they took Selkirk by surprise. When Selkirk was safely locked in the Pike County jail, the McCoys must have felt that a traitor at last had received his just deserts.[10]

The day after the arrest of Selkirk McCoy, Phillips wrote to Governor Wilson on the official stationery of Attorney Perry Cline. In his capacity as agent of Governor Buckner, Phillips stated that Kentucky did not care about extradition of Elias Hatfield and Andrew Varney. He enclosed fifteen dollars, however, for warrants for Devil Anse, Johnse, and Cap Hatfield, Daniel Whitt, and Albert McCoy, the son of Selkirk. Some of those named in the indictments had since died, and the Kentucky authorities reasoned that if they wanted any of the others yet living they could send for warrants later.

Another obstacle blocked Phillips's path. On December 17 Wilson, with characteristic hot temper, responded to Phillips's letter of December 13 by stating that information had reached him that "certain parties have received a large sum of money from parties named in the requisition." The governor coupled his rather oblique statement with a curt reminder that "the money for fees should be sent to the secretary of state—not to me. I herewith return the fifteen dollars, and shall make enquiry into the matter." He declared, rather ominously, that "requisitions and warrants thereon are issued to subserve the ends of justice and for no other purpose."[11]

Wilson had good reason for misgivings about the extradition of the Hatfields and others to Kentucky. An ugly rumor had reached him that Perry Cline had induced Governor Buckner to advertise large rewards for the capture of the West Virginians and had then extorted money from the Hatfields in return for a promise that he would use his influence with the Kentucky governor to bring about a compromise. Wilson, whose honesty and integrity matched the quickness of his temper, had no intention of contributing to such double-dealing.

Still later Wilson heard that the Hatfields, through an attorney, had offered to stay out of Kentucky if Governor Buckner would withdraw the requisitions and that Cline had endorsed their offer. A. J. Auxier, a Pike County attorney who had been engaged by some of those under indictment for the murder of the McCoys, corroborated the rumor on December 22. In a signed affidavit, he stated that following the announcement of the rewards for the arrest of Devil Anse Hatfield and others, the Hatfields had provided him with money to be used to pay fees and expenses in connection with the effort to induce Buckner to withdraw the rewards. Auxier declared that the Hatfields had specified that part of the money—$225, he believed—should be paid to Cline to reimburse him for his alleged expenditures toward that end. According to Auxier, Cline had written the secretary of state of Kentucky urging acceptance of the conditions proposed by the Hatfields.

More damaging evidence emerged concerning the motives and actions of Cline. G. W. Pinson, the clerk of the Pike County Criminal Court, swore that he had copied the indictments against the twenty West Virginians for Cline in order that Cline might induce Governor Buckner to offer rewards for their arrest and to make a requisition upon the governor of West Virginia for their delivery.

Johnse Hatfield added details of the agreement with Cline. In a statement affirmed before John A. Sheppard, a notary public of Logan County, West Virginia, Johnse declared that he, with Auxier and James York, attorneys for the Hatfields, visited Cline in December 1887 and came to a verbal understanding with him. Johnse confirmed the earlier assertion of Auxier that the Hatfields had paid Cline $225 in return for which he was to endeavor to stop the proceedings for the arrest of Devil Anse and the others. He further stated that "it was well understood at the time of the making of said agreement by all parties interested that . . . Cline had not spent any such sum of money in the manner stated by him, but that it was only an excuse for him to take shelter behind."[12]

Whatever satisfaction the Hatfields might have gained from the promise of Perry Cline must have been at least partially offset by the address of Governor Buckner to the Kentucky legislature on the last day of December 1887. Sensitive to the adverse publicity which disorders in the mountain counties had brought to Kentucky, Buckner pointed out that "the reputation of a community is often popularly judged by the conduct of its worst elements" and that "the law-abiding character of the people of Kentucky [was] estimated by others, in a great measure, not from the general disposition of its citizens to obey the laws, but from the violent conduct of comparatively a few lawless individuals." Buckner declared, "If, from neglect or inefficiency, we fail to repress this lawlessness, or to bring the offenders to justice, we have no right to complain of the false estimation in which we are held by the people of other states."[13]

Although the press of Kentucky hailed the governor's address as holding out a promise of action against those who flouted the laws of the state, the Hatfields looked upon it as a threat. To them, it gave added evidence of collusion between Governor Buckner and men such as Perry Cline, whom they now considered the epitome of duplicity. If the governor attempted a serious assault upon the lawlessness in the eastern counties, the Hatfields indeed had reason for apprehension.

7

NEW YEAR'S DAY 1888

Until the autumn of 1887 the Hatfield-McCoy feud remained primarily a family vendetta, waged without effective intervention by the constituted authorities of either Pike or Logan counties. The election of Governor Buckner and his support of the proposals of Perry Cline, however, lifted the feud into the political sphere. Although Buckner's motives were unquestionably altruistic, his intercession did not herald a new evidence of the majesty of the law or of swift and certain justice. Rather, through the machinations of Cline and his associates, it resulted in an infusion of the cheapest and most corrupt kind of politics. Other feuds of the Kentucky mountains had repeatedly shown that when legal authority failed to stand above the warring factions and arrayed itself on one side or the other, it intensified and prolonged the troubles. Without any doubt, the politicization of the Hatfield-McCoy feud and the efforts of Cline to turn it to personal advantage forced it into one of its most violent periods.

Although the Hatfields had no confidence in Cline and other Kentucky authorities and little expectation of justice, much less of mercy, at the hands of a Pike County court, they might have done well to allow matters to settle for a time. Already Governor Wilson's reaction to the letter of Frank Phillips and the reports of Cline's venality held forth the possibility that he would not honor the extradition request from Kentucky.

Moreover, the exposure of Cline's duplicity might have undermined some of his influence with Governor Buckner. The threat remained, nevertheless, that Pike County friends of the McCoys or bounty hunters might engage in extralegal methods to arrest the Hatfields and take them to Kentucky for trial. The Hatfields had no intention of allowing that to happen.

Early in the morning of a cold, crisp January 1, 1888, Devil Anse, Jim Vance, and Cap Hatfield decided to take the initiative. They dispatched Johnse and Tom Chambers, also known as Tom Mitchell, to round up the clansmen, some of whom, either because of fear of arrest or a desire to avoid further entanglement in the feud, were hiding in the hills. Johnse's wife, Nancy, had left him, and he was temporarily free to participate in the activities of his family.

The first recruit was the easily influenced Ellison Mounts, reputedly the son of Ellison Hatfield. Over six feet tall and weighing more than 180 pounds, the twenty-four-year-old Mounts seemed the archetype of the wiry, athletic mountaineer. With his light blond hair and dull gray eyes, he was generally called "Cotton Top." His boyhood had been spent "in the usual pursuits of a rude, unrully [sic] country boy, in fishing, hunting, roving about the neighborhood and engaging with boon companions in Sabbath-breaking, petty pilfering, and all the multifarious pursuits known to the average ungoverned country boy." Barely literate, his "education in vice" had been "very thorough," and he participated in his first murder in 1882 after the McCoy brothers killed his father in the election-day troubles on Blackberry Creek.[1]

At Dow Steele's, on Island Creek, Johnse, Chambers, and Mounts met Devil Anse and his sons, Cap and Robert E. Lee, or Bob, who was a mere youth. According to Mounts, they continued on to the homes of Henry Vance, Floyd Hatfield, and other supporters and finally arrived at the cabin of Jim Vance. There Devil Anse, Cap, and Vance held a council and presumably came to the conclusion that they must eliminate Randolph McCoy and members of his family who might present damaging evidence against them if they were extradited to Pike County for trial. As Jim Vance explained, with agreement from Cap and Johnse, the Hatfields had "become tired of dodging the officers of the law, and wished to be able to sleep at home beside better bed fellows than Winchester rifles, and to occasionally take off their boots when they went to bed."

Once the plans were announced, the men unanimously expressed their willingness to participate in them. Ironically, the only one to hold back was Devil Anse, who declared that he was too sick to take part and that he would turn over the leadership to Vance. No one questioned the sincerity of Devil Anse's explanation, and all agreed to accept Vance as their leader. Altogether, eight men placed themselves at Vance's command. They included Cap, Johnse, Bob, and Elliott Hatfield, the last a son of Ellison and a nephew of Devil Anse, Tom Chambers, Ellison Mounts, Charles Gillespie, and French, or Doc, Ellis. Vance sought to impress upon his followers the importance of absolute fidelity to the plan. Raising his arms above his head, he declared, "May hell be my heaven; I will kill the man that goes back on me tonight, if powder will burn."[2]

With unity and firmness of purpose, the band of nine well-armed men advanced up the Tug Fork. Between four and five o'clock in the afternoon they stopped at Cap Hatfield's for supper. Darkness was coming on fast, but a full moon appeared. Concealing themselves as much as possible, the men proceeded to Poundmill Run and crossed a ridge to Peter Branch and Blackberry Creek. Their route, almost identical to that taken by Wall Hatfield and the Mahon brothers the night following the attack upon Ellison Hatfield by the McCoys, undoubtedly brought back bitter memories and steeled them in their resolve to remove a potential threat to them. Passing Jerry Hatfield's, the site of the fateful 1882 election, they swung up Hatfield Branch to the crest of a mountain and emerged on Blackberry Fork of Pond Creek. When they had gone about a mile, they tied their horses, and Cap, Johnse, and Vance put on masks. From there they advanced silently toward Randolph McCoy's house, which stood on a flat of heavily wooded hillside.[3]

According to the plan of attack, the nine men surrounded the McCoy dwelling, a double log house with a roofed passageway connecting the two parts. Cap and Mounts stationed themselves at the back door of the kitchen, and Bob and Elliott Hatfield covered the kitchen door that opened upon the passageway. Johnse and Vance watched the entrance from the passageway to the main house, and Chambers, Gillespie, and Ellis stood guard over the front entrance.

After they had taken their positions, Jim Vance called for the McCoys to come out of the house and surrender as prisoners of war. His demand awakened Calvin McCoy, the twenty-five-year-old son of Randolph, who was sleeping in the upstairs of the main part of the house. Calvin hastily put on his trousers and suspenders and hurried downstairs to warn his mother to remain quietly in bed. He then went back upstairs for a better vantage point for defense, while his father took up a position on the first floor.

About that time Johnse, ignoring the orders of Jim Vance to withhold fire until he gave the signal, shot into the McCoy house. His precipitous action was followed by a fusillade from the attackers and answered by rapid firing by the McCoys from the windows, with Calvin "shooting like lightning." Ironically, the first victim of the encounter was Johnse, who received a charge of bird shot in the shoulder.

In the midst of the shooting, Jim Vance and Tom Chambers undertook to set fire to the house. Vance ran to a side of the building that had no windows, where he saw some cotton drying. He struck a match to it and placed part of it in a joist hole and the remainder against the shutter of the door. Chambers, observing the new tactic, dashed to the woodpile and seized a large pine knot, which he ignited. With the blazing pine knot, he ran to the kitchen area, where he leaped upon a pile of logs and onto the roof. There he attempted to pry loose a shingle, with the intention of placing the burning pine knot in the loft.

Before he could accomplish his purpose, someone fired a gun from the room below, blowing a hole in the roof and momentarily blinding Chambers. When he regained his composure and his sight, he saw that his numb and bloody hand had three fingers missing. He dropped the torch, rolled to the ground, and sped off as fast as he could to safety. The pine knot fell to the ground and smoldered harmlessly.

The fire that Vance had ignited at the door of the cabin, however, showed signs of spreading rapidly. Calvin McCoy called to his sisters, Josephine, Alifair, and Adelaide, to put it out, but Vance warned that if they came out he would shoot them. The girls tried to extinguish the flames with the water in the cabin, which they quickly exhausted, and then used the buttermilk in the churn, but to no avail. The fire spread and began to engulf the doorway.

About that time Alifair opened the kitchen door. She beheld the masked men but called out to Cap Hatfield that she recognized his voice. Cap and Johnse saw her at the same instant and called to Ellison Mounts, who was nearest her, to shoot her. Mounts fired and the girl collapsed on the ground near the doorway. Josephine called from the inside to ask whether her sister was hurt, but the incomprehensible moans of Alifair left no doubt that she had been mortally wounded. Sensing some tragedy, Calvin called down to find out what had happened. His answer came in Josephine's screams that the attackers had killed Alifair.

Upon hearing that Alifair had been shot, Sarah McCoy, her mother, rushed to the back door. Vance commanded her to go back and raised his rifle as if he would shoot her too. Sarah saw, however, that he had the wrong end turned toward her and continued toward her dying daughter. Vance bounded toward her and struck her with the butt of the rifle. For a moment she lay on the cold ground, stunned, groaning, and crying. Finally, she raised herself on her hands and knees and tried to crawl to Alifair.

According to Sarah McCoy's own account, she pleaded with the attackers, "For God's sake, let me go to my girl." Then, realizing the situation, she cried, "Oh, she's dead. For the love of God let me go to her." Sarah put out her hand until she could almost touch the feet of Alifair. Running down the door-sill, where Alifair had fallen, was blood from the girl's wounds. Johnse, who was standing against the outside wall of the kitchen, took his revolver in the hand which he could still use and beat Sarah over the head with it. She dropped to the ground, face down, and lay motionless.

Meanwhile, the fire continued to spread along the front and one side of the larger cabin. By then nearly overcome with smoke and realizing that the situation for the family was desperate, Calvin descended the ladder to the lower story and told his father that he would make a run for the corncrib and hold off the attackers while Randolph tried to run past them to safety. Calvin never made it to the corncrib. Surmising his plan, the Hatfields concentrated a murderous fire upon him, and he, too, met his death.

Calvin's bold scheme enabled Randolph to escape from the burning house. Grabbing extra cartridges, the older man, still vigorous at sixty-two years of age, dashed through the smoke and into the nearby woods. Knowing that pursuit would be foolhardy, the Hatfields had to content themselves with a mission only half-accomplished. In their frustration, they set fire to the McCoy smokehouse, which was filled with fresh meat from the fall slaughtering. They retired from the scene, blaming Johnse's impetuous firing for the failure of their plan and certain that the wrath of Randolph McCoy would now know no limits. Their new venture and the survival of witnesses left them more vulnerable than ever.[4]

Dejected, the Hatfield party mounted their horses for the ride home. Charley Gillespie's horse had broken loose during the attack, and he rode behind Cotton Top Mounts, who fainted from the loss of blood on the way. From the ridge above Blackberry Fork they could see the burning cabin and the trees outlined against the reddened sky. Faintly, in the distance, they could hear the wails of the McCoy girls, crying for help in their distress.

Behind them the Hatfields left a scene of unmitigated horror. Calvin and Alifair lay dead, and Sarah McCoy remained unconscious. When Randolph McCoy emerged from a pigpen, where he had taken refuge, he saw that his daughters Adelaide and Fanny, who were seventeen and fourteen years old, had built a small fire to protect their apparently dying mother from the penetrating cold. Randolph found Sarah with her arm and hip broken and her skull crushed. He saw the dead bodies of Calvin and Alifair, the latter with her long hair frozen to the ground. Even a less vindictive man than he might have vowed revenge at such a sight.

Shortly afterward neighbors, attracted by the fearsome nighttime fire, arrived at the McCoy homestead. They placed Sarah on a cot and carried her to the home of her son Jim, who lived about a mile farther down Blackberry Fork. A few days later they bore the bodies of Calvin and Alifair to the McCoy cemetery, where they laid the two most recent victims of the feud to rest beside their three brothers—Tolbert, Pharmer, and Randolph, Jr.—who had been buried in a triple grave less than six years earlier.[5]

Left without a home and with sorrows and hatred weighing upon him, Randolph McCoy left Blackberry Fork. He moved Sarah, still valiantly clinging to life, by wagon to Pikeville and to the home of Perry Cline. There they found Rose Anna, who made the care of her mother her own reason for living. Two pictures of Randolph during the succeeding weeks have emerged. Truda McCoy describes him as a silent, morose, and broken man. Virgil C. Jones, however, states that, in contrast to the women of the family, who bore their grief in silence, "the wails of the father were uncontrolled" and that he frequented the streets of Pikeville cursing the Hatfields and threatening revenge. Perhaps both descriptions contain some truth, as both appear to be in keeping with aspects of McCoy's character.[6]

The violence of New Year's night of 1888 diverted some of the attention of the newspaper press from other feuds of the Kentucky mountains. Attracted by the sensational aspects of the events, but lacking reliable information, the press seized

with avidity upon grossly inaccurate and often totally un-
founded rumors. The *Louisville Courier-Journal* of January 8,
1888, like other Sunday newspapers of the week following the
attack upon the McCoy family, carried a brief account based
upon a letter written to State Senator A. H. Stewart by a
friend in Pikeville. The *Courier-Journal* declared, "It appears
that in 1882 parties led by a man named Hatfield, abducted
three boys named McCoy, and conveyed them to West Virginia. A reward was offered for the arrest of the Hatfield party,
and one of the gang was captured, who is now in the Pike
County jail. On Sunday last others of the same party went to
the residence of Randolph McCoy, in Pike County, and killed
his wife, mother of the three boys mentioned, and his son,
also set fire to the house, which, with its contents, was entirely
consumed."

The newspaper article further stated, "Two little girls,
daughters of McCoy, escaped, and succeeded in recovering
the dead bodies from the flames. McCoy escaped in his night
clothes under fire of the murderers, shooting as he went, but
without effect so far as ascertained." The account noted, "The
Pikeville jail is strongly guarded, but fears were entertained at
the hour of writing that an attempt would be made to release
the member of the gang [Selkirk McCoy] confined there."

Although it provided more accurate background material,
the *Wheeling* (West Virginia) *Intelligencer* of January 9, 1888,
drew upon a dispatch from Catlettsburg, carried by the *Cincinnati Enquirer*, for an equally erroneous version of the attack upon the McCoy dwelling. "A few nights since," the dispatch stated, "the Hatfield party visited the residence of Randolph McCoy and set fire to the house. Alafara, his eldest
daughter, was the first to open the door and make her appearance, and in the glaring light she was shot dead by the fiends
outside, who were concealed. His son Calvin next appeared,
and he was shot dead. His wife made her appearance in escap-
ing from the burning building and was shot through the head,
and although she was still alive at last accounts she will die."
Adding to the errors and simplifications, the account further
declared, "Randall M'Coy escaped from the burning house

with his shotgun, and although a volley was discharged at him he escaped unhurt, and opened fire upon the attacking party. He is known to have killed one of the gang by the name of Chambers, and, it is said, shot Cap Hatfield in the shoulder, and putting the rest to flight. So ends the chapter."

The *Intelligencer* added that $2,700 in rewards had been offered for members of the Hatfield clan charged with the murders of the three McCoys in 1882 but that "no one seems anxious to take them, as they are strongly barricaded in the wilds of West Virginia." Declaring that the outlaws had killed McCoy's wife, three of his sons, and a daughter, the writer also speculated that "retributive justice is now likely to follow, as their last acts have stirred up that whole section," but he observed that "if the Hatfields are ever taken, dead or alive, the men who undertake the job will experience some fun, as this set of West Virginia toughs is a determined and desperate band."

Remoteness from the scene of the tragedy only partly explained the inaccurate stories carried by the press. One of the most erroneous accounts appeared on January 12, 1888, in the *Big Sandy News* of Louisa, Kentucky, the closest newspaper. It reported that it had received "reliable information" from Pikeville that "Cap Hatfield was killed and that John[se] Hatfield and other members of the gang were badly wonded [*sic*] by Calvin McCoy and his father." It declared that Calvin "mortally wounded two of the squad before he was killed." The article also carried the mistaken news that "A seventeen-year-old daughter of McCoy [Adelaide] has become insane over the awful affair" and that "One of Johns [*sic*] Hatfield's arms was so badly lacerated and shattered that it has been amputated." After the type for the article was set up, the editor added later information to the effect that Cap had not been killed, but he injected another error by declaring that Chambers, rather than Selkirk McCoy, was then under heavy guard in the Pikeville jail.

Just as Perry Cline's activities introduced a political dimension to the Hatfield-McCoy feud, so the Hatfield attack upon the McCoys on the night of January 1, 1888, placed it in the journalistic sphere. The newspapers proved no more able than the politicians to bring truth to the surface and to promote a resolution of the turmoil that beset Pike and Logan counties. Yet, in the long run, both contributed to a conviction by the people that, for the good of the two states, the mountain dwellers would have to settle their differences by more peaceful means.

8

THE HATFIELDS
ON THE DEFENSIVE

With much of Pike County seething with anger over the events of the night of January 1, Randolph McCoy demanded that Sheriff Harmon Maynard take action, but Maynard declined to go into West Virginia without extradition papers. Frank Phillips, however, was of different mettle. Sensing the support of the people and posing as a state agent armed with full authority, he organized a band of some twenty-seven men for a foray into Hatfield territory.[1]

Expecting a new effort on the part of Governor Buckner to extradite them to Kentucky, the principal leaders of the Hatfield clan took oaths before Justice of the Peace Joseph Simpkins that they were nowhere near the McCoy residence on the night of the attack. They hoped that affidavits setting forth plausible alibis would prevent Governor Wilson from honoring any requisition for their extradition. Devil Anse apparently felt deep concern for the fate of his two stalwarts, Cap, who, according to most accounts, had killed Alifair McCoy, and Jim Vance, who had beaten up her mother. Rumors also circulated that the three chief leaders of the Hatfields had attempted to save Cap and Vance by paying Ellison Mounts five hundred dollars for a confession that he had killed Alifair.[2]

Frank Phillips and his posse caught the usually wary

Hatfields off guard. They concentrated their first efforts upon Cap and Jim Vance, who had gone to Vance's home. The two men remained there longer than they had intended because Vance had become ill after eating raccoon meat, which his wife, Mary, had prepared. They set out for Cap's residence, with Mary Vance walking along the trail ahead of them. At the crest of a hill, she shouted that she saw Phillips and "a whole passel" of men on the other side. Vance directed Mary to continue on, and he and Cap took cover behind large rocks. When Phillips and his men came near, they opened fire, emptying their guns in rapid succession to give the impression that they had several others with them. Phillips, also knowledgeable in the ways of mountain fighting, was not deceived. He and his posse spread out, and one of his men got a clear line on Vance and shot him in the stomach. Vance at once commanded Cap to flee to safety.

Taking no chances with the sly Vance, Phillips and his men closed in with caution. Phillips walked up to Vance and fired a bullet into his head. Newspaper accounts of the incident, based upon misinformation, reported that not only Vance but also Johnse Hatfield and Tom Chambers had lost their lives in the encounter.[3]

Following the death of Vance, the leaders of both sides pursued a policy of guarded aggressiveness. Phillips and his posse returned to the hills of Kentucky and ventured into West Virginia only in brief, daring raids. The Hatfields, as anticipated, swept up and down the banks of the Tug Fork but did not cross the river lest they provoke the dispatch of state troops into Logan County or alienate Governor Wilson.

On January 19 the opposing forces met in pitched battle on Grapevine Creek, a West Virginia tributary of the Tug Fork. Phillips and some eighteen men had returned to West Virginia for another raid when they encountered thirteen Hatfield partisans, led by a constable, J. R. Thompson, armed with a warrant for the arrest of the murderers of Jim Vance. The two parties rushed for cover behind rocks and began to fire furiously. The first man wounded was Bud McCoy, regarded as one of the most dangerous of his clan. Soon afterwards the

McCoys claimed their first victim, young Bill Dempsey, who suffered a shattered leg. Dempsey crawled into a shuck pen and was calling for water when Phillips, Dave Stratton, Jim McCoy, and three other men began to abuse him. The youth told them that the sheriff had summoned him as part of a guard to pursue the Kentuckians, whereupon Phillips walked up close to Dempsey, "drew his revolver and shot his brains out with one shot."[4]

Newspaper accounts embellished the battle of Grapevine Creek. Inaccurate and based upon the flimsiest of rumors, they informed readers that Phillips and his associates had robbed Dempsey of a silk handkerchief and $2.50 which he had in his pocket when he died; that Jim Vance's killers had shaken hands over his dead body; and that Randolph McCoy had sent Cap Hatfield word that he intended to kill him, cut out his heart or a piece of flesh, and broil and eat it. The *Wheeling Intelligencer* declared that if "one half of the stories of brutality and murder are true, the case would seem to warrant the authorities of both states in taking hold and ending the trouble, even if it is necessary to call the state troops into action."[5]

Despite the gory accounts in the press, Frank Phillips had reason for gratification. In his forays into West Virginia he and his men captured Wall Hatfield, a Logan County justice of the peace, Tom Chambers, Elias Mitchell, Andrew Varney, L. S. McCoy, a son of Selkirk, Moses Christian, Sam Mahon, Dock Mahon, and Plyant Mahon, who joined Selkirk McCoy in the Pike County jail. The Hatfields were stunned by the depletion of their ranks, and West Virginia offered rewards for the capture of Phillips and twenty-one members of his posse.[6]

The hostilities of the early weeks of 1888 broke up the already crumbling marriage of Johnse Hatfield and Nancy McCoy. Johnse, always one of the weakest of the Hatfields, could not resist the pressures to join them in their moves against the McCoys, and Nancy, high-spirited and determined, always remained loyal to her family. When they parted, Nancy returned to Kentucky with their two children. In time she went to Pikeville, where she met Frank Phillips, who had separated from his wife. Nancy and Frank found at once that they were kindred spirits and began to live together. About two months later, when they received their divorces, they were married.[7]

Meanwhile, Rose Anna began to falter. She continued to care for her mother, who had fainting spells and needed assistance in walking, but she herself grew more and more depressed. Sarah McCoy sent for a doctor, who found nothing wrong with her daughter. Rose Anna, however, continued to lose ground, and one day she slipped away into death, much to the shock of residents of Pikeville. Her family laid her to rest in the Dils Cemetery in Pikeville. Rose Anna, perhaps as much as her sister and four brothers who rested in graves on Blackberry Creek, was a victim of the feud with the Hatfields.[8]

In late January 1888 Pike County Judge Tobias Wagner and County Attorney Lee Ferguson, both instrumental in action by the state the previous autumn, went to Frankfort and requested Governor Buckner to protect the lives and property of Pike County residents. Buckner listened attentively to their plea, but he professed to see no provocation sufficient to justify the dispatch of state troops to Pike County. He advised that its citizens organize a local militia force, with responsible men in command, and expressed the opinion that this force, backed by civil authorities, would be adequate to deal with the situation.[9]

About the same time a delegation from Logan County presented Governor Wilson with a petition, signed by some of the most prominent men of the county, calling upon him either to provide troops to defend them or arms with which they might protect themselves. The petition drew attention to the recent deaths of Jim Vance and Bill Dempsey at the hands of desperados from Kentucky and pointed out that Dempsey was a sheriff's deputy who was killed while attempting to discharge his official duties.[10]

Spokesmen for residents of Pike and Logan counties maintained that the disturbances involved more than a hard-core of feudists in the Hatfield and McCoy families. S. G. Kinner, the commonwealth attorney for the Sixteenth Judicial District of Kentucky, declared that each side in the feud then had about thirty men, most of whom were among the best people of their sections. He pointed out that the Hatfields were men of means and standing in their communities but noted for vindictiveness, while their Pike County adversaries included "as good people as you will find anywhere." State Senator John B. Floyd of Logan County denied that the conflict was confined to the two families and contended that it had become essentially one between the civil authorities of Logan County and the murderers of Jim Vance. He declared further, "The Hatfields are not interested in the difficulty more than other citizens of Logan County and, while the McCoys are among the Kentucky men, they constitute but a small portion of the gang."[11]

Floyd, whose family had been closely connected with the Hatfields and who himself lived for twenty years within eighteen miles of the principal feudists, also provided a history of the trouble between them and the McCoys. His account, printed in the *Wheeling Intelligencer* on January 27, 1888, stressed the Civil War origins of the vendetta. After detailing some of the main events in the increasing hostility between the two families, including the killing of Ellison Hatfield and three sons of Randolph McCoy, Floyd laid the blame for the resurrection of the troubles, which most people thought were over, squarely upon Perry Cline. He charged that Cline had deliberately looked up the old indictments against the Hatfields after six years and induced the governor of Kentucky to offer $2,700 in rewards in order that he might extract money from the well-to-do Hatfields as a price for getting the rewards withdrawn.[12]

While elements on both sides of the Tug Fork sought some political settlement of the Hatfield-McCoy trouble, newspapers continued to whip up public excitement with sensational articles. The *Pittsburgh Times* found events along the Kentucky-West Virginia border of sufficient interest to dispatch a correspondent, Charles S. Howell, to the scene. Howell spent three days in Pike County and returned with a one-sided version of the feud which he touted as a definitive account. Published as a five-column feature in the *Times* of February 1, 1888, his article contained more than a score of serious factual errors and highly garbled accounts of the troubles growing out of the election of 1882, the killing of Jeff McCoy, and other incidents in the feud. Reproduced in numerous other journals, his account did much to color popular views of the vendetta.

Howell succeeded in obtaining interviews with Randolph and Sarah McCoy and with the Hatfield partisans who had been captured by Frank Phillips and lodged in the Pike County jail. Howell had deep sympathy with the McCoys, whom he visited at their house in Pikeville, which he found almost devoid of furniture. The couple, he declared, showed "unmistakable evidences of the intensity of their sufferings." Contrary to most descriptions of Randolph, he pictured "a man who had been bent and almost broken by the weight of his afflictions and grief," but who had only once given any thought to retaliation. He quoted McCoy as saying, "I used to be on very friendly terms with the Hatfields before and after the war. We never had any trouble till six years ago. I hope no more of us will have to die. I'll be glad when it's all over."

Howell painted a very different portrait of Devil Anse, whom he never saw. The leader of the Hatfield clan emerged as an absolute monarch who brooked no challenge to his authority and who cold-bloodedly embarked upon a war of extermination of the McCoys without any real provocation. The newspaperman blamed Devil Anse and his associates for the Hatfield-McCoy war, which he characterized as "simply a succession of cowardly murders by day and assassinations and house-burnings by night."

Nor did Howell form a more favorable opinion of the West Virginians whom he visited in the Pikeville jail. "The prisoners," he declared, "are good types of their locality. Old 'Wall' Hatfield is a tall, powerful, well-proportioned man. He has iron gray hair and moustache to match, while a pair of rough, shaggy eyebrows almost conceal eyes of a greenish gray that are forever evading the eyes of the person with whom their owner may be talking. Cool and self-possessed at all times, 'Wall' never allows himself to be led into making any entangling statements." The Mahons, two of whom were Wall's sons-in-law, he reported as masters of "bravery and cunning." Howell noted that Wall had not participated in the attack of January 1, 1888, and had advised against it. His refusal to take part had allegedly produced a breach between him and Devil Anse.

Howell evinced considerable admiration for both Frank Phillips and Perry Cline. "Frank Phillips has made himself so conspicuous in his efforts to capture and suppress the Hatfield gang," he wrote, "that he has been removed from his position as Deputy Sheriff. The Sheriff of Pike County is Basil Hatfield, a connection of the heads of the Hatfield gang, and himself is charged with giving them aid and comfort in removing Phillips and substituting his own. Phillips, however, has been appointed agent of the Governor of Kentucky to recover the Hatfields, for whom requisitions were issued. He says he will capture them all eventually and do all in his power to bring about their punishment." Howell described Cline as "the demon of the prosecution" and a man "prolific of resources, patient, brave and untiring."

In concluding his story, Howell declared, "There is a gang in West Virginia banded together for the purpose of murder and rapine. There is also a gang in Kentucky whose cohesive principle is the protection of families and homes of men and women. An unresisting family has been deprived of five of its members, a father and mother of five of their children, their homes burned, their effects sent up in smoke, their little substance scattered to the wind, themselves forced out at midnight as wanderers on the bleak and inhospitable mountain side, almost naked in the blasts of winter. A mother stands by and sees her son killed before her very eyes without being allowed to speak to him. Farms are destroyed, religious meetings are broken up, men and women whipped, state and county elections interfered with and terror holds complete sway. To repress the gang that has committed all these crimes was the Kentucky gang organized. These are the gangs, their respective histories, objects and achievements."

Newspaper accounts such as that of Howell undoubtedly exacerbated feelings of hostility between the two states in which the feud occurred. Even before the publication of Howell's one-sided account, the *Wheeling Intelligencer* noted that, "with one or two exceptions, all the press dispatches relating to the matter which have appeared, have been sent from Kentucky towns." It further declared that they had "a decided coloring in favor of the McCoy faction, and are evidently calculated to make it appear that the Hatfields are the aggressors. Pains are taken in the accounts sent out by these Kentucky corespondents [*sic*], also, to create the impression that the affair is a case of 'West Virginia outlawry,' much to the discredit of the State. The truth of the matter is that it is a Kentucky feud, and is the result of a difficulty which occurred at a local election between the rival factions in Pike county, Kentucky, some years ago." The *Intelligencer* contended that there had been nothing in the events to justify such distortions by the press, which reflected unfairly upon West Virginia.[13]

By the end of January 1888 most of the blood in the feud had already been shed. What until then had been a vendetta between two relatively obscure Tug Valley families was by then, however, in the process of becoming an interstate cause célèbre, a windfall for muckraking newspapers and magazines, and a conspicuous element in the legendry of the southern Appalachians.

9

THE GOVERNORS
INTERVENE

Events along the Tug Fork in January 1888 almost inevitably drew the governors of Kentucky and West Virginia more deeply into the problems relating to the feud. On January 9 Governor Buckner wrote Wilson that he had received reports of the attack upon the McCoys on the night of January 1 and inquired whether there was any good reason why the men indicted for the murder of the McCoy brothers in 1882 should not be rendered to Kentucky.[1]

Because of sickness in his family and his absence from office with the Board of Public Works, Wilson did not reply to Buckner's letter until January 21. He reminded Buckner that more than five years had elapsed before any application had been made by Pike County officials for extradition of the men charged with the murder of the McCoys, that those charged had lived in the vicinity continuously, and that the application for requisition had not been supported by any official authority of Pike County. Nevertheless, he had directed the issuance of warrants for all the persons named with the exception of Elias Hatfield and Andrew Varney. Wilson suggested that "neither [Perry] Cline nor [Frank] Phillips, nor any of the persons engaged in the recent violations of the law, are proper persons to entrust with process of either Kentucky or West Virginia." He requested Buckner to make further inquiry in order that warrants might be issued only against those for whom there was some evidence of guilt.[2]

News of the battle of Grapevine Creek reinforced Wilson's decision to defer compliance with the request for extradition. He wired Buckner on January 25 that he had received information that "William Dempsey was killed while acting as deputy in assisting the officers of the law in arresting Frank Phillips and three of the McCoy boys on a warrant for the murder of James Vance." Dismissing a return wire from Buckner, which stated that Buckner's information differed from that of Wilson and that steps were being taken to prevent any aggression by Kentucky citizens upon those of West Virginia, Wilson, on January 26, addressed a letter to Buckner with further details. He declared that he now had "positive information" corroborating facts set forth in his earlier message to Buckner.

Taking a position that constituted a strong endorsement of the Hatfield claims, Wilson wrote Buckner, "Recently the hope of reward has prompted a set of men quite as lawless as either the Hatfields or McCoys to the commission of heinous crimes against the laws of this state and upon its citizens while discharging their duty as officers of the law." He stated that he had been unofficially informed that a number of West Virginians had been forcibly seized and taken from the state by a band of Kentuckians and confined in the Pike County jail. He told Buckner that he had sent a reliable agent to Logan County to ascertain the facts and expressed the hope that Buckner would follow a similar course in order that they might concert measures for the suppression of lawlessness on both sides of the Tug Fork.[3]

In response to Wilson's letter, Buckner wrote that he had sent Kentucky Adjutant General Sam E. Hill to Pikeville and had instructed him to confer with Wilson's agent, Colonel W. L. Mahan, with a view to quieting the situation along the borders.[4] In the meantime, both governors ordered their state troops to stand by for possible service on the Tug Fork. The Kentucky State Senate debated a bill for the addition of six new units to the State Guard. With lukewarm interest, it considered several proposed amendments, one of which would have struck out a provision for sending guns to the counties in which the troops would be stationed and inserting a statement that "six good school teachers and two evangelists be sent to said counties, to remain until the disturbances are quelled." Although both the governor and the adjutant general recommended passage of the militia bill, with the understanding that one unit would be sent to Pike County, the House of Delegates defeated the measure. Upon receipt of a petition from Logan County, Wilson called out the Goff and Auburn Guards of Ritchie County, who entrained at Pennsboro with the expectation of arriving in Charleston on January 31.[5]

Shortly after Wilson sent his letter to Buckner, Mahan returned from Logan County with confirmation of Wilson's assessment of the situation along the Tug Fork. Mahan reported that he found the Hatfields "good, law-abiding citizens," who were respected in their neighborhood, and that the recent outbreak of violence had been caused by the resurrection of the old indictments against them by certain persons in Kentucky. He told Wilson that Kentuckians had crossed the Tug Fork into West Virginia and "kidnapped" nine men, killed Vance "without as much as calling on him to surrender," and slain William Dempsey. Most residents with whom Mahan had talked believed that if the arrest of the Hatfields had been assigned to persons other than the McCoys, who "had sworn to kill the Hatfields and would have done so after they were disarmed," no blood would have been shed. The Hatfields, he stated, simply could not trust their safety to McCoy partisans. On the strength of Mahan's report and in the belief that the clans had disbanded their forces, Wilson notified Buckner on January 30 that he had countermanded his order directing troops to Logan County.[6]

Kentucky Adjutant General Hill did not reach Pikeville until after Mahan had returned to Charleston. His investigation seemed to confirm the description that Mahan had given to Governor Wilson. Unlike Mahan, however, Hill concluded that responsibility for the disturbances lay with West Virginia rather than Kentucky and that former state senator John B.

Floyd had obstructed justice by urging the governor to ignore the requisitions by Kentucky. Hill also reported that he had visited Perry Cline and found him a man of great courage. He failed to mention that Cline was accompanied at all times by three guards armed with Winchesters and revolvers.[7]

On January 30, several days before Hill returned to Frankfort, Buckner wrote Wilson a long letter in which he placed the blame for the troubles on the Hatfields and expressed surprise that there should be any delay in rendering to Kentucky men who now stood guilty of the perpetration of "other crimes of the most atrocious character in the same locality." He insisted that extradition procedures had been in proper order and that Wilson should issue warrants for Elias Hatfield and Andrew Varney and allow the courts to determine their guilt rather than pass judgment himself. Buckner admitted that Cline had tried to persuade him to withdraw the rewards for the Hatfields in return for their promises not to come to Kentucky again. He drew attention away from the corruption of Cline, however, and raised questions about the means used by the Hatfields to prevent the requisitions and rewards from being honored. Finally, Buckner justified the delay of Pike County officials in seeking extradition on the somewhat irrelevant ground that the indicted men were so heavily armed when they were in Pike County that officials dared not arrest them.

Frank Phillips, Buckner stated, had sent the required fee for extradition to West Virginia and had gone into that state only when he had no acknowledgment from Wilson. With two other persons and "without any disturbance or conflict of any kind," he had succeeded in capturing Tom Chambers, Selkirk McCoy, and Moses Christian, three of the men named in the indictments. Phillips had transported his captives to Kentucky and lodged them in the Pike County jail. According to Buckner, that action had prompted the attack upon the McCoy family on the night of January 1, 1888. Following the brutal assault upon the McCoys, Phillips, with a company of armed men, made three expeditions into West Virginia. The first resulted in the killing of Vance, the second in the capture of six additional West Virginians, and the third in the encounter in which Bill Dempsey was killed.

Confessing the difficulties in ascertaining the facts of the situation along the Tug, Buckner stated that he had obtained his information from Lee Ferguson, the county attorney of Pike, who had taken great pains to get at the truth. Buckner expressed regret that any citizens of Kentucky had attempted to arrest West Virginians without first obtaining proper authority, but he reiterated his conviction that "Frank Phillips . . . is not the murderous outlaw your excellency seems to suppose." He added, however, that "as he had undertaken to arrest some of the parties in West Virginia without your warrant, and is, therefore, objectionable to you, I will, when your excellency indicates your readiness to surrender the persons demanded, take pleasure in designating another agent for that purpose."[8]

Convinced that West Virginia had more reason for complaint than Kentucky and that further correspondence with Buckner was pointless, Wilson decided to institute legal proceedings against Kentucky. On February 1 he dispatched Mahan to Frankfort with a request that Governor Buckner immediately release the nine West Virginians, who had been seized illegally. He instructed Mahan to obtain an answer from Buckner before he returned to Charleston. Less than a week later Mahan brought a letter from the Kentucky governor explaining that the courts, not he, had jurisdiction over cases involving the release of prisoners.[9]

Regarding Buckner's response unsatisfactory, Wilson decided to initiate habeas corpus proceedings. Passing over his attorney general, Alfred Caldwell, who allegedly warned that West Virginia had at best a weak case, he engaged Eustace Gibson, a prominent Huntington attorney, who had served as Speaker of the West Virginia House of Delegates and member of Congress, to present the case to the United States District Court in Louisville. On February 8 Gibson presented the petition to Judge John Watson Barr, who set a hearing for noon the next day, with Gibson and former governor J. Proctor Knott of

Kentucky representing their respective states. In his motion for writs of habeas corpus, Gibson stated that armed men from Kentucky had invaded West Virginia without warrant, legal authority, or legal process and taken West Virginia citizens to the Pike County jail, where they faced great danger of assassination. In addition, the motion charged that armed men had captured Selkirk McCoy while correspondence between the governors of the two states was in progress.

Kentucky Attorney General Parker Watkins Hardin, who had been directed to appear at the hearing, declared that he had received only a few hours' notice and asked additional time for preparation. Gibson expressed a desire to be courteous, but he contended that the trial should be held as soon as possible to protect the lives of the prisoners, which he claimed to be in jeopardy. Although professing sympathy for the prisoners, Hardin questioned the jurisdiction of Judge Barr's court over the matter and refused to consent to the writs until he had time to study the matter. Gibson agreed to a short postponement, and the court recessed until ten o'clock on February 10.[10]

When the court reconvened, Gibson opened the arguments by noting that the case had no precedent, since the federal government had never had to deal with a situation in which one state demanded that another surrender its citizens who had been illegally seized. He held that a requisition could be made only under the United States Constitution, which, though it might not assure protection to the states, guaranteed American citizens protection against unlawful seizure.

Knott took the position that the case was not one between the states but involved a simple question of whether writs of habeas corpus should be issued to bring certain criminals to justice. He vigorously defended the course pursued by Governor Buckner in the Hatfield-McCoy matters and contended that even an illegal capture of the Hatfields could not prevent their confinement in the Pike County jail, since they were guilty of the gravest of crimes. Knott argued that if Gibson's reasoning prevailed any criminal could escape prosecution and find safety in another state. He denied that the lives of the prisoners were in danger and asserted that they could expect a fair trial in Pike County.

Hardin maintained that if the points at issue involved the states, only the United States Supreme Court had jurisdiction. He denied that such was the case, however, and contended that when Wilson asked for the writs of habeas corpus, he, in effect, became before the law a person and not the governor of West Virginia. Only the prisoners themselves, he contended, could ask for their own release. On a practical note, Hardin declared that if the court liberated the West Virginians they would return home and never face trial for their crimes.

Gibson presented the closing arguments. He defended the actions of Governor Wilson and held that Buckner had evaded the issue in his letters to Wilson. He suggested that the failure of Kentucky to seek extradition of those charged with the murder of the McCoy brothers for more than five years after their indictments constituted bad faith. On a note of sarcasm, he declared, "With all the magnificent power of this State [Kentucky]—with all the power of her executive, her judiciary, her army that has been so often called on to protect her Judges from assassination by her citizens, or the citizens from assassination by the Judges—with all this power, for five years Kentucky took no steps to bring those indicted men to justice until a shyster lawyer named Kline [sic] brought up the subject and caused the Governor to offer the magnificent reward of $2,500 for the capture of men who had stood with arms outstretched ready to be taken." Finally, Gibson drew a graphic picture of the mountain warfare in Kentucky, which he declared not only a disgrace to the state but also to the nation and which, he said, had no counterpart in West Virginia.

Judge Barr summed up the case. He accepted the contention of Hardin that it was not essentially one between the two states and that his court therefore had jurisdiction over it. He dwelt upon laws relating to habeas corpus and provisions protecting the rights, liberty, and property of individuals. He found nothing to show that the West Virginians had been legally arrested and confined to the Pike County jail, although he conceded that the issuance of bench warrants may have legalized their arrest once they crossed the state line. Although Barr held that all the men involved should have signed the petition for the writs of habeas corpus and given the grounds for their suit in writing, he overlooked the technical error and, after some demurral by Hardin, made the writs returnable on February 20. He ordered the jailer of Pike County to produce the nine men in court at Louisville.[11]

Reaction of the press to Judge Barr's decision was predictable. The *Louisville Courier-Journal* on February 12 declared, "For years the press and the officers of the state have been earnestly endeavoring to make the law a terror to evildoers, and now for the first time in the history of any civilized community the power of a 'sovereign state' is invoked to give protection, license, and immunity for the past and assurances for the future to a band of white savages whose brutalities, whose inhuman tortures have not been paralleled in Kentucky since Boone and his followers drove the Indians to other hunting grounds." On the other hand, the *Huntington Advertiser* on February 18 extolled the services of Gibson, who "did honor to himself and to the State in the matter of the application for the writ." The *Advertiser* considered the "savage tone" of the *Courier-Journal* regarding Barr's decision a measure of Gibson's success.

Governor Wilson acted immediately upon the decision of Judge Barr. Two days later he issued a requisition upon Governor Buckner for twenty-eight men, all charged with participating in the murder of William Dempsey. His requisition produced no immediate result, since Buckner did not comply with it, but it served as an indication that for the moment the initiative in the Hatfield-McCoy troubles had passed from Kentucky to West Virginia.

VICTORY FOR KENTUCKY

THE DAY AFTER Judge Barr rendered his decision, United States Deputy Marshal J. V. McDonald left for Pikeville to serve the writs of habeas corpus. Contrary to the dangers depicted by Eustace Gibson in his arguments before Judge Barr, the marshal found the town of Pikeville quiet. Rumors persisted, however, that the Hatfields would try to rescue the prisoners. For that reason, a carefully chosen guard, under the direction of Perry Cline himself, accompanied them to Louisville. The guard included Lee Ferguson; Jim York, the attorney for Randolph McCoy; Charley Yoste, a deputy sheriff of Pike County; Jim Sauers, first lieutenant, and Allen Cline, second lieutenant, of the Pikeville militia; and Link Cline and Dan Marrs. The guard conducted the prisoners to Catlettsburg and placed them aboard a Chesapeake and Ohio Railway train. On the evening of February 16, at 7:15, they arrived in Louisville.[1]

A reporter for the *Louisville Courier-Journal*, who hurried to Catlettsburg and made the journey with the prisoners, obtained interviews and provided curious readers with details of their experiences. Wall Hatfield impressed the reporter as a mild, quiet, and intelligent man. He steadfastly denied any knowledge of the killings for which the men had been indicted. According to Wall, Kentucky officials asserted that the

West Virginians, who had been seized by armed men from Pike County, had been arrested after they reached Kentucky.

Jail officials, Wall stated, had treated the men well, and he himself had not been locked up, although all the prisoners remained under heavy guard because of fears of attempts upon their lives or efforts to rescue them. He told the reporter that Perry Cline had declared that he would never give up the West Virginians and that Randolph McCoy, who had allegedly threatened to shoot Wall on sight, had said that he could not desire the Hatfields in a better place than the Pike County jail. Wall declared that he had tried to give bond and that Colonel John Dils had offered fifty thousand dollars as surety, but Pike County officials had refused to release him.[2]

To the large crowd of curious people who gathered at the Louisville railroad station, the prisoners appeared very different from the mountain folk frequently brought to the city on moonshine charges. All wore soft felt hats, several of them chose white shirts, and at least three had on collars. Mostly young men, they appeared indifferent as they walked at a brisk pace and under heavy guard to the jail. Within half an hour after the train arrived they were in the custody of federal marshals.

The reporters then turned their attention to Lee Ferguson, who proved a special delight. The loquacious Ferguson insisted that the West Virginians were guilty of the crimes charged against them and that the Kentucky posse was justified in forcibly taking them from their homes. He ventured the information that one West Virginia official, meaning John B. Floyd, had received a fee of five hundred dollars from the Hatfields to prevent Governor Wilson from honoring the extradition request from Kentucky. Ferguson also told the reporters that Devil Anse had sold five thousand acres of land along the Tug Fork for seven thousand dollars, despite its worth of at least fifteen thousand, and moved near Logan, some forty miles from the border. Finally, he added the titillating story that Wall Hatfield had five living wives and thirty-three children and that he did not marry the wives according to law, but apportioned his time among them.

For several days the Hatfields remained the center of interest in Louisville. The *Courier-Journal* of February 17 devoted most of its front page to a feature that included an artist's drawings of the nine prisoners and Randolph McCoy. Other inmates of the jail developed a fondness for the West Virginians, who soon dropped their initial reticence and began to converse freely. They especially liked Wall, whom they nicknamed "Judge." The Hatfields in turn enjoyed the reading which other prisoners did for them and took part in divine services, particularly the singing of hymns, which they rendered with remarkably fine voices. They proved unable, however, to adjust to the schedule of the other inmates and continued their mountain practice of going to bed at dusk and arising noisily between four and five o'clock in the morning.[3]

Judge Barr called the habeas corpus case for Saturday morning, February 25. To the spectators who filled the courtroom, the Hatfields and their associates presented a stoical appearance throughout the proceedings. After seemingly endless debate between the attorneys for the two states, Barr recessed the court until Monday, February 27. When it resumed, Governor Wilson and his close associate, John B. Floyd, armed with books and official records, joined Gibson and his associate, J. W. St. Clair. The small, slender Wilson, who nibbled almost constantly at his bushy red mustache, conferred frequently with the West Virginia attorneys and impressed those present as a remarkably able man.

The counsel for the Commonwealth of Kentucky based their arguments upon the claim that a prisoner could not escape prosecution by pleading illegality or irregularity of arrest; that Frank Phillips had acted as an individual and upon his own responsibility and not as an agent of the Commonwealth in arresting the West Virginians; and that Kentucky was not responsible for his actions or those of the men who accompanied him. Citing a number of cases to support their points, Hardin and Knott maintained that the violation of proper procedures did not suspend the right of a state to arrest a wanted person found within its borders.

Gibson insisted that the cases cited by Hardin and Knott did not apply to the issue at hand. In none of them, he declared, had prisoners been deprived of their liberty until they have been found by an officer with proper authority to confine them. The Hatfields, on the other hand, had been held for more than twelve hours before the legal execution of warrants upon them. Gibson maintained that Phillips himself had stated that he acted under the authority of Kentucky and accused the Pike County prosecuting attorney of summoning all the magistrates as witnesses to prevent them from hearing the case. Finally, he charged the attorneys for Kentucky with "mere fiddling."

At the conclusion of the arguments, Judge Barr declared that he could not render a decision at once. The case had no precedent, and he needed to consult constitutional authorities. Before leaving the courtroom, St. Clair drew the attention of the judge to Wall Hatfield, whom he described as an aged man in poor health. St. Clair stated that the confinement and prison food had caused Wall to become ill and that he needed medical care. Barr promised that Wall should have whatever assistance he required.[4]

On March 3 Barr announced his decision. In essence he held that the question involved a controversy between two states and therefore lay beyond the jurisdiction of his court. Under the Constitution, only the Supreme Court had jurisdiction. He thereupon remanded the prisoners to Kentucky authorities. He rejected a request by Gibson that they be allowed to give bail, holding that the offense with which they were charged was not bailable. Pending a decision as to which jail they should be confined, Barr ordered them locked up for the night.

Before Barr adjourned the court, Andrew Varney made a request. "Judge," he said, "I wanna go back to Pike." When the astonished judge inquired, "Why?," Varney answered, "Cause, the court thar are gonna be aholden for a week, an' I wanna go back and show I ain't guilty." Barr reminded Varney, "If you had not made application for a writ of habeas corpus, you would be there now." Varney's answer was even more astounding than his original remark. "It warn't on my account I were brought here. I didn't know nothin' 'bout it till I got here." Barr could only observe, "I wish I had known that before" and try, as did the attorneys, to conceal his bewilderment.

Eustace Gibson castigated some of the procedures in the case as reprehensible. In an interview with reporters at the Galt House, where he had accommodations, he stated his belief that someone had tampered with some of the prisoners. Moreover, he declared, he did not "think much of either Governor Knott or Attorney General Hardin, both of whom have been contrary and unaccommodating throughout the trial."[5]

On Monday, March 5, Wilson, who had returned from a temporary absence from the city, filed an appeal. The argument before Judge Barr became heated, and Wilson asked to be sworn in as an attorney. He tried unsuccessfully to have the letters he had received from Frank Phillips and Perry Cline introduced as evidence, but Knott vigorously protested and Barr denied the request. Wilson based his major argument for an appeal upon the ground that the case must decide whether kidnapping constituted a legal means of arresting citizens, particularly, as he emphasized, when the kidnappers engaged in collusion with authorities of one state to bring to trial persons residing in another. That afternoon Barr granted the appeal and ordered the prisoners held until Pike County officials returned for them.[6]

Wilson and Gibson bent their efforts toward preventing trial of the prisoners in Pike County and their removal to the jail there, where, they contended, their lives were not safe. The *Louisville Courier-Journal*, in a scathing and ungracious editorial of March 6, maintained that the prisoners would not only be safe in the Pike County jail but that they would receive a fair trial, since "the courts of Kentucky are not apt to convict innocent men." Referring to an argument in court over responsibility for the costs incurred in conveying the prisoners to Louisville, the editorial repeatedly referred to the "sovereign but impecunious" state of West Virginia and commiserated with the prisoners, who, it asserted, might have to pay their own expenses.

Nearly ten days passed before Perry Cline arrived in Louisville for the prisoners. By then not only had West Virginia refused to bear the expenses of their journey to Louisville, but the United States marshal had also refused to accept responsibility. Cline, therefore, interrupted his plans to go to Frankfort, where he persuaded Governor Buckner to seek a special appropriation from the Kentucky legislature for the costs involved. On March 16 he returned to Louisville and arranged for the journey back to Pikeville.[7]

While the West Virginians remained in Louisville, Wall Hatfield continued to attract reporters. He steadfastly maintained that not a single man among them had anything to do with the murder of the McCoy brothers. Instead, he fastened the guilt upon Devil Anse and his sons, Cap, Johnse, and Bob, and four or five others. With a sense of humor, he then expressed the wish to one reporter that his newspaper would retract a printed report that Wall had seven wives. "I ain't never had but one," declared Wall, "and I don't want any more."[8]

After some disagreement over whether the appeal of the habeas corpus case should go directly to the United States Supreme Court, Judge Barr ruled that it should follow regular procedure and be heard in the United States Circuit Court. With the prisoners no longer on hand, the case presented in the Circuit Court before Judge Howell E. Jackson had little of the drama of that heard in Judge Barr's court and attracted relatively little attention.

On April 5 Eustace Gibson opened the testimony by reviewing the evidence presented at the earlier trial. He again emphasized the wrongs done the prisoners through their illegal seizure, which constituted a violation of the Constitution of the United States. Knott admitted that the West Virginians had been taken from their state illegally, but he denied that the mode of their apprehension in any way affected the legality of their arrest once they were in Kentucky. He declared that the arguments of the opposing counsel seemed to imply that "the Constitution of the United States was drawn expressly to give each state the power to harbor criminals." Governor Wilson even alluded to the possibility of war between two states. Hardin expressed no desire to speak. Judge Jackson, who had to remind all the speakers to confine their remarks to the issue in question, granted the appeal of the case to the United States Supreme Court.[9]

On April 13 Gibson and Knott, who had served together in the United States House of Representatives, arrived in Washington to present the cases of their respective states. The attorneys succeeded in having the Supreme Court advance the case, know as *Plyant Mahon, appellant* v. *Abner Justice, jailer of Pike County, Ky.*, on the docket and began their arguments on April 23. Speaking for one hour and thirty minutes, Gibson held that the "taking and holding" of Mahon (and inferentially of the other eight men) "was one continuous act by the same officers of the State of Kentucky," and "the act of Phillips in capturing and Cline in locking up in jail without warrants of mittimus, were both wrongful acts of the State of Kentucky." Knott, who spoke for only about twenty minutes, maintained that the question was one of law and in no way a case between the states. Had it been, West Virginia should have instituted her suit in the Supreme Court, which had original and exclusive jurisdiction, and not in the District Court.[10]

A reporter for the *Wheeling Intelligencer* noted a general opinion that West Virginia's procedures had been "wrong from the beginning" and that Wilson had "applied at the wrong shop for redress." West Virginia, it was feared, might be "kicked out of the Supreme Court on the question of form, without reference to the merit of her case—and it is conceded that the merit was great." The reporter cited a common belief that if the case came before the Supreme Court in proper form the West Virginians would win their freedom, although they might later be rearrested under legal circumstances.[11]

The Supreme Court, in an opinion presented by Justice Stephen J. Field, upheld the judgment of the lower court. The opinion held that although the arrest and abduction of Mahon (and, of course, the others) were "lawless and indefensible acts," the "authority from the Governor of Kentucky furnished no ground for charging any complicity on the part of the State in the wrong done to the State of West Virginia." The opinion maintained that no legal means existed whereby a person accused of a criminal offense in one state could be turned over to authorities in another state except through positive law on the subject.[12]

Justices Joseph P. Bradley and John M. Harlan offered dissenting opinions in which they stressed the view that the court should have recognized the invasion of West Virginia by Kentucky. Bradley expressed the opinion that the writs of habeas corpus had been properly issued and that Mahon (and the others) should have been discharged and permitted to return to West Virginia. He further declared that Mahon "was kidnapped and carried into Kentucky in plain violation of the Constitution of the United States, and is detained there in continued violation thereof." He held that the Constitution "clearly implies that there shall be no resort to force" for the purpose of apprehending persons charged with crime and fleeing into another state and that it had, in fact, "abrogated, and the States have surrendered, all right to obtain redress from each other by force."[13]

Once the Supreme Court rendered its decision on the arrest and confinement of the West Virginians, attention reverted to the prisoners themselves and to others who had been indicted for the McCoy murders but remained at large. That the men confined in Pikeville would be brought to trial and that Kentucky authorities would redouble their efforts to apprehend those still at large was a foregone conclusion.

11

HAWKSHAWS
IN THE HILLS

DURING THE WEEKS following the decision of the Supreme
Court, detectives arrived in Kentucky and West Virginia from
all parts of the nation. They hoped to collect the rewards offered by Kentucky for the Hatfields and by West Virginia for
the McCoys, which by the summer of 1888 totaled almost
eight thousand dollars. Some of them aspired to the fame that
might come from capturing the principal feudists, particularly
Devil Anse.

The wily mountaineers took precautions against capture by
ambitious and unscrupulous detectives. None did more to in-
sure his safety than Devil Anse. Shortly after the attack on the
McCoys on the night of January 1, 1888, he purchased two
tracts of land, of 200 and 250 acres, on Island Creek, a tributary of the Guyandotte River.[1] He built a cabin near present
Stirrat, West Virginia, about midway between his old home
near the mouth of Peter Creek and present Logan. He chose a
site in a narrow valley between two ridges that extended down
the highest mountain between Logan and the Kentucky border, a location so isolated that "people with no business there
knew instinctively that they should stay away, and those
whose duties called them to the lonely valley went in trepida-
tion."[2]

In withdrawing from his lands along the Tug Fork, Devil

Anse made a major concession to the reduction of tensions, but he had no intention of surrendering to Kentucky authorities. Some distance from his cabin he erected another structure designed as a fortress for use in case the McCoys sought further retaliation or legal authorities or detectives tried to take him and his supporters by force. Built of twenty-three-foot logs almost two feet in diameter, the building had only one entrance, with a massive solid oak door nearly twelve inches thick and capable of stopping bullets of the most high-powered Winchesters. Portholes in all walls enabled defenders to fire in any direction. Devil Anse stocked the fort with adequate food and water, as well as sufficient fuel for the large fireplace, against the time when he and his friends might have to take refuge there and endure a long siege.[3]

Devil Anse formed a cadre of well-armed men prepared to assemble at the fort on short notice. They included Cap, who had returned from a trip to the western states, which he had involuntarily taken following the battle of Grapevine Creek. Devil Anse also laid in a supply of arms and ammunition, newly purchased from the manufacturers. Although his purpose was purely defensive, news of the purchases aroused fears in Pikeville that the Hatfields might attempt a rescue of the prisoners in jail there. Captain C. M. Parsons of the Buckner Guards, Pikeville's newly organized militia unit, appealed to Kentucky Adjutant General Sam E. Hill for aid and received in response a generous supply of ammunition.[4]

Meanwhile, West Virginia authorities took legal initiatives of their own. At its spring term of 1888 the Logan County Circuit Court indicted Frank Phillips, Deputy Sheriff John Yates of Pike County, Bud McCoy, James McCoy, David Stratton, and twenty-three others for the murder of Jim Vance. Governor Wilson promptly offered rewards of five hundred dollars for Phillips and one hundred dollars each for the other twenty-seven men. During the summer of 1888 most of those under indictment in both Kentucky and West Virginia remained in hiding in the woods and left the care of their farms to their women and children.[5]

Both the Hatfields and the McCoys held the detectives in

contempt. The editor of the Louisa *East Kentucky Magnet* voiced a commonly held opinion that it did not matter to them "whether they arrest a McCoy or a Hatfield just so they see a few dollars in the transaction." He proposed, "Hang the detectives, drive off all who are not residents, and those most concerned will soon find that it is safe and profitable to attend to crops and get their timber ready for the spring rains. Offer rewards for the detectives, and enough honest Hatfields and McCoys will unite to clear the country of them in less than two weeks. When the Hatfields and McCoys realize the injustice that is done them, and the opinions held in regard to them by the outside world, and all brought about by the workings of detectives, they will make it so hot that, if any of them (the detectives) escape, they will bury their bought badges and swear that they never heard of the Big Sandy country."[6]

On June 1, 1888, Captain Alfred Burnett of the Eureka Detective Agency and two assistants left Charleston, West Virginia, for the Tug Valley. The primary object of their journey was the arrest of Dave Stratton, who had been with Frank Phillips at the time of the killing of Bill Dempsey. The detectives proceeded to the mouth of Pigeon Creek, a West Virginia tributary of the Tug Fork, and from there to Blackberry Creek, on the Kentucky side. Two of them called at the house of Stratton at the mouth of Knox Creek and learned that he was flatboating. They combed both sides of the Tug and about daybreak on June 22 found Stratton asleep on a sandbar just inside the West Virginia border. They approached him with great stealth, and when they were near him one of them leaped astride him and pushed the barrel of his revolver against Stratton's head. Resistance being useless, Stratton surrendered peacefully. The detectives took the Winchester rifle and the Colt revolver, which he carried, and escorted him to the Logan County jail.[7]

Most of the detectives had no encounters with the feudists, and many of the rumors emanating from the Tug Valley probably grew out of efforts to cover up their lack of success. One of the stories involved a man known as William L. Minyard. Reputedly from the Indian Territory, Minyard dressed in imitation of Buffalo Bill Cody and called himself "Wild Bill." He claimed that he concentrated his efforts upon the capture of the McCoys and that on one occasion he barely escaped capture himself by hiding in a hollow log while Frank Phillips and a band of McCoys searched all about for him. Unfortunately for him, he was arrested on charges of peddling moonshine, which he contended in vain was part of his plan for taking the McCoys.[8]

On July 23 detectives of the Eureka Agency, along with "Wild Bill" Minyard and a stranger, arrived in Charleston and claimed rewards for the arrest of two of the McCoy partisans. They reported "a sharp fight" at the mouth of Peter Creek in which one member of a band of some thirty McCoy supporters had died and several others were wounded, but otherwise they were "very close-mouthed" about matters on the Tug. Perhaps more action was generated when Eustace Gibson, the West Virginia attorney in the habeas corpus case, and the editor of the *Saint Marys* (West Virginia) *Oracle*, came to blows in Parkersburg over the congressional election of July 25.[9]

Reports persisted that several Hatfields, including Devil Anse, Cap, Elias, and Tom Chambers, fearing that the large rewards would lead to their arrest, had left or were leaving the state. Police at Roanoke, Virginia, reported several Hatfields quietly moving northward along the Norfolk and Western Railway, and newspapers warned readers that they were desperate men who would not give up without serious trouble. Most rumors credited the McCoys with being ahead of the Hatfields in the new phase of the feud in the summer of 1888.[10]

Despite the stream of rumors, the hills along the Tug remained relatively quiet. Judge W. H. Weddington of the Pike County Criminal Court, annoyed over newspaper reports that any unknown person in Pike County would be shot, declared, "Strangers are in no more danger here than they would be in Frankfort or Lexington." Moreover, he stated, "The McCoys are all pursuing the peacable [*sic*] avocations of life, while the Hatfield party who are not in jail in Pikeville are fugitives in the mountains of West Virginia." Ignoring the fact that Frank Phillips had taken up with Nancy McCoy Hatfield, Johnse's wife, Weddington stated that the Pikeville attorney and agent of Governor Buckner was living as a private citizen on a farm about ten or fifteen miles from Pikeville.[11]

Reporters, nevertheless, continued their unflattering descriptions of mountain life. A staff writer for the *New York Sun*, sent to Logan County ostensibly to report on the hunting situation, declared, "The presence of detectives has made the criminals exceedingly cautious, and that means that they are ready to shoot an armed stranger on sight, not to mention the temptation they would feel to become possessed of the sort of weapon a Northern sportsman would be likely to carry." The Hatfields, who visited Logan one day in mid-August to collect royalties for mineral rights they had sold to eastern capitalists, asserted their intention of remaining peacefully at home and, as Judge Weddington observed, disturbing no one unless they were molested.[12]

In August 1888 T. C. Crawford, a much-traveled reporter for the *New York World*, visited Logan County in the company of John B. Floyd and Clarence Moore of the United States District Court at Charleston, whom he persuaded to accompany him. At Logan they met Elias, a brother of Devil Anse. With his broad forehead, deep-set, clear blue eyes, large Roman nose, and determined chin, Elias resembled his more famous brother. Although he appeared reticent and nervous, he revealed a decisiveness of character. He gave the appearance of a man of restraint but with peculiar ideas regarding killing. "All I want," he declared, "is to be let alone. But if people keep on botherin' and wrongin' those who are dear to me—why, let them look out."

Farther on, Crawford and his companions saw in the doorway of a cabin a man described by the newspaperman as "unprepossessing, unhung a villain as I have ever had the misfortune to see. He had a small, bullet head, frosty complexion, washed-out eyes, little pug nose and great sandy mustache lining the cruel, tight-lipped mouth. He balanced a Winchester across his lap." Crawford learned later that the man was

French Ellis, one of the participants in the attack upon the McCoys the previous January.[13]

A few hundred·yards farther on the travelers met Devil Anse himself. The feud leader impressed Crawford with his powerful frame, broad shoulders, and deep chest. Although about fifty years old, he had no gray in his hair, beard, or bushy eyebrows. His nose was hooked "like a Turkish scimitar." Devil Anse wore a brown coat, faded black hat, blue shirt, and blue jeans, the latter tucked into his high boots. When his coat swung open, Crawford noticed that he carried a large Colt revolver strapped to his hip in addition to the rifle which he had with him.

Devil Anse proved so cordial and hospitable that Crawford found no difficulty in asking rather personal questions relating to the feud. To the observation that Devil Anse was said never to have killed anyone "for the pleasure of it," the patriarch answered, "I ain't that kind o' man." He vowed, however, to protect his family against all danger. Asked what he would do if a detective tried to capture him, Devil Anse answered without hesitation, "Wall, now, I ain't aimin' t' be bothered no mo'. I been hidin' out in th' brush an' kept 'way from my bebbies." On the other hand, he stated flatly, "I want this trouble settled. It's gone on long 'nuff. I aim t' stay at my home, whar I am, fur the present. If th' Guv'ner sends a paper hyar fur me in th' right form, why, I ain't a-gonna kill th' man whut brings it."

Devil Anse told Crawford that he had nine men on guard constantly and that he did not intend to surrender. He declared that he might hide out in the woods, "an' I reckon nobody kin ketch me in these hyar mountins. I jist ain't a-gonna be taken." Devil Anse spoke indulgently of the McCoys and expressed regret that the feud had occurred. The reporter left the clan leader convinced that many of his people might yet die but that it would take half a regiment of soldiers to capture them.[14]

In early autumn the Hatfields suffered a further depletion of their ranks. On October 14 the *Cincinnati Enquirer* reported that for more than three weeks Charles Gillespie, one of the men wanted for the McCoy family murders of 1888, had been confined to the jail in Ironton, Ohio. "A handsome fellow, presumably nineteen years old, with dark hair and eyes, very gentlemanly in appearance, and . . . the last man one would point out as a desperate man," Gillespie had been traced for months by detectives, anxious to take him dead or alive. About September 15 Detective P. A. Campbell of Wellston, Ohio, captured him in Virginia. When Campbell got the drop on Gillespie, thrust his revolver a few inches from the young man's head, and ordered him to throw up his hands, Gillespie answered coolly, "You've got me dead to rights; shoot if you want to, but recollect a Hatfield never throws up his hands. Treat me like a man, though, and I'll go quietly with you."

On the way from Virginia to Wellston, Ohio, Campbell and his prisoner stopped for several days at the home of Detective Alf Burnett in Charleston. Gillespie adamantly refused to divulge any information to Burnett, but he found Mrs. Burnett a kindly woman, and "in a burst of confidence, he told her his story." When they arrived in Wellston, Gillespie again gave an account of his part in the feud to Campbell's wife, who wrote it out and had Gillespie swear to it in the presence of the mayor of the town. Shortly afterward, Campbell took Gillespie to the jail in Ironton. There Gillespie remained until Lee Ferguson, the commonwealth attorney for Pike County, and Burnett arrived with requisition papers from the governor of Kentucky and removed him first to the Catlettsburg jail and then to Pikeville.

At Catlettsburg, Gillespie received a visit from Charles S. Powell, the indefatigable reporter for the *Pittsburgh Times*. Once again Gillespie related his story, which had wide circulation not only in the *Times* but in other newspapers as well. He told Howell that he had been lured into accompanying the Hatfields in the New Year's venture into Kentucky by Cap, who promised some fun. He identified Cap, Johnse, Elliott, and Bob Hatfield, Jim Vance, French, or Doc, Ellis, Ellison Mounts, Tom Chambers, and himself as the participants in the attack upon the McCoy family. The object of the attack, Gillespie quoted Jim Vance as saying, was to kill Randolph

McCoy and his son Calvin and thereby remove "every material witness against the men who had taken part in the murder of the three McCoy boys." By eliminating the witnesses, the Hatfields hoped to prevent their own conviction even if they were brought to trial. Gillespie reiterated a remark made by Vance that the Hatfields and their friends wanted to sleep without the necessity of keeping their rifles at hand and constantly fearing arrest. Gillespie stated that the attackers decided that if the McCoy family would not come out when called, they would shoot through the windows and doors until all inside were dead. According to Gillespie, he and one of the Hatfields had no part in the killings but simply stood guard some distance away until the house was burning.[15]

Before the end of October Detectives Dan Cunningham and Treve Gibson captured Ellison Mounts. They tracked Mounts assiduously for days and finally ambushed him on a road near the head of Mate Creek. Unlike Gillespie, Mounts proved an unwilling captive, and several shots were fired before the detectives got him in handcuffs. During the exchange Mounts shot Gibson in the leg.

After they captured Mounts, Cunningham and Gibson concentrated their attention upon Alex Messer, one of the most dangerous men in the Tug Valley. Messer had once served as deputy sheriff of Perry County and allegedly had twenty-seven notches in his gun. With the same diligence they had shown in apprehending Mounts, the detectives traced Messer to a store in Lincoln County, West Virginia. They engaged him in friendly conversation, and Messer invited them to his lodgings. There Cunningham and Gibson identified themselves, and the helpless Messer went along peacefully.[16]

The Hatfields knew that they could not tolerate further decimation of their ranks by the detectives. Unfortunately for their continued success, the detectives talked much too freely. Some of them, including Dan Cunningham and Dick Evans, boasted around Logan that they had plans to shoot Devil Anse, Cap, and French Ellis after which they anticipated no trouble in capturing the remaining Hatfields. On January 12 the Hatfields swore out peace warrants for the garrulous detectives.

Soon afterward, the Hatfields caught them and marched them to the Logan jail. To add insult to injury, the Hatfields climbed on the backs of the detectives each time they had to ford a stream and forced the hawkshaws to carry them across.[17]

The resentment felt toward the detectives appeared in a letter to the *Logan County Banner*, allegedly written by a neighbor but more likely by one of the Hatfields. An arsonist, believed to have been Dan Cunningham, set fire to Devil Anse's barn and crib, causing the loss of a horse valued at $150 and 150 bushels of corn. Regarding the incident, the writer declared, "I think it is an outrage and disgrace to the public to let such go on. We want peace in our land and country, and not destruction of property by fire and trying to kill and destroy what the people have worked and made by the sweat of their brow. Anderson Hatfield is as peaceable a man as we have in Logan County, if he is let alone. . . . Now we ask the detectives to not interfere with our business and we will not interfere with them."[18]

Hostility toward the detectives long continued. Several years later William G. Baldwin, the head of the Baldwin-Felts Detective Agency, went to Island Creek to track down one of the Hatfields engaged in making moonshine. Posing as a simple traveler, he thought that he scored something of a coup by spending the night with Devil Anse, who extended his usual hospitality. About four o'clock the next morning, however, Devil Anse called the astonished Baldwin by name and told him that breakfast was ready. Then, telling the detective that he had some mean boys who might harm him, he escorted Baldwin to the top of a distant ridge, and the outwitted detective was forced to leave empty-handed. The Hatfields, despite their enmity, might have some respect for the McCoys; for the detectives they had none.[19]

12

THE HATFIELDS
STAND TRIAL

IN LATE AUGUST 1889 the trial of the Hatfields and their associates for the McCoy murders opened in Pikeville. Before it commenced, Lee Ferguson, the commonwealth attorney for Pike County, extracted a confession from Ellison Mounts, whom detectives had captured in October 1888 and whom Ferguson regarded as the weakest member of the Hatfield clan. Mounts admitted that he had participated in the murder of the three McCoys on the night of August 9, 1882. He provided an account of their detention at the schoolhouse on Mate Creek, identified Charles Carpenter as the man who tied the brothers to the pawpaw bushes, quoted Devil Anse as advising them to make their peace with God, and named Devil Anse, Johnse, Cap, and Bill Tom Hatfield, Carpenter, Alex Messer, and Tom Chambers as those who actually shot the McCoys. Mounts confirmed the story that Wall Hatfield swore the participants in the murder to secrecy. He also described the shooting of Jeff McCoy, as told to him by Cap Hatfield.[1]

Besides the confession of Mounts, the prosecution produced nineteen witnesses. The presence of eight witnesses who bore the name of Hatfield serves as a forceful reminder that the division between the Hatfield and McCoy clans was not nearly as sharp as many writers have portrayed. Randolph McCoy, who took the witness stand first, testified that he was with his sons when Wall Hatfield and his supporters overtook the Pike County officers en route to Pikeville and persuaded them to turn their prisoners over to the Hatfields. Randolph proved a disappointing witness in that his memory of many incidents appeared hazy and unreliable.

Sarah McCoy, on the other hand, had a vivid recollection of the night of August 9, 1882. She gave details of her visit to the schoolhouse on Mate Creek, where she saw Cap, Johnse, and Bill Tom Hatfield, Carpenter, Messer, Dan Whitt, and others, all of them armed. She remembered Wall's stating that if Ellison Hatfield died, they would shoot the McCoy brothers as full of holes as a sifter bottom. She also recounted her conversation with Wall at the house of Perry Cline in Pikeville, but she did not recall telling him that her son Tolbert had mentioned kind treatment by Wall during the time that the McCoys were held or that he had asked his friends to be kind to "Uncle Wall."

James McCoy, the forty-year-old son of Randolph and Sarah, added details to those provided by his parents. Jim remained at the schoolhouse on Mate Creek until news came that Ellison Hatfield had died. He then started back to his brothers and on the way met Wall and Elias Hatfield, Plyant Mahon, and Elijah Mounts, whom he saw again at the mouth of Sulphur Creek "at thick dusk" heading toward Mate Creek. About twenty minutes later, from Asa McCoy's house near the mouth of Sulphur Creek, he heard about fifty shots, which he believed came from the Kentucky side of the Tug Fork. Jim and several others later went to the scene of the shooting and found his three brothers dead. He declared, under cross-examination, that he had talked with Wall Hatfield in the Pike County jail in 1888, but he had no recollection of telling John Scott that Wall had nothing to do with the murder because he did not have time to get to the scene after Jim had seen him at the mouth of Sulphur Creek.

The testimony of most of the other witnesses corroborated that of Randolph, Sarah, and James McCoy in essential outlines. Joe Davis asserted that it was he who informed Wall Hatfield that young Randolph McCoy, Jr., had cut Ellison

Hatfield and that Wall had said that was all he wanted to know. Dan and Jeff Whitt turned state's evidence in return for a promise by Commonwealth Attorney S. G. Kinner that he would dismiss indictments against them. Dan Whitt stated that at the time of the trial he was staying with "Uncle Randall McCoy," but that he had talked "but little with him or Aunt Sallie about this case." Both Whitts testified that Wall had sworn those present at the killing of the McCoys to secrecy regarding the murders on penalty of being hanged. Several witnesses, including Sam McCoy and Floyd Hatfield, testified that they had heard Wall declare that if Ellison died the McCoys would be killed but that otherwise they would be turned over to the proper authorities. Several discrepancies appeared in the testimony of the witnesses, one of the most glaring being in that of the Whitt brothers, who disagreed on whether Plyant Mahon or his brother Sam was among four men who left the scene of the shooting before the murder of the McCoys took place.

On the witness stand, Wall Hatfield had the appearance of a man in mortal fear of an unfavorable verdict. He gave details of the manner in which he learned of the attack upon Ellison and the arrest of the McCoys. He traced his subsequent actions in overtaking the officers conducting the McCoys to Pikeville. Wall explained his insistence that the McCoys stand trial in the district in which the altercation occurred as deriving from his desire to obtain testimony from Dr. Jim Rutherford and his Uncle Valentine, also called Wall, Hatfield.

Wall described the journey to the Reverend Anderson Hatfield's residence and Devil Anse's command to friends of the Hatfields to fall in line, but he could not remember crossing the river with the Hatfield party. Insisting that all he ever wanted was a civil trial for the McCoys, he maintained that while he was at the schoolhouse on Mate Creek he had tried in every way to prevent harm to the McCoys and that he had never told Randolph McCoy or any other person that if Ellison died or if a rescue or ambush party appeared the McCoy brothers would be shot. He admitted asking Joe Davis whether he had seen young Randolph McCoy cut Ellison, but he emphatically denied that he had administered any oath of secrecy to those present after the killing of the McCoys.

Although he admitted that he "did not visit the Ky. side very much," Wall declared that he never made any effort to avoid arrest. He stated that he wrote Perry Cline that he desired to surrender and that before his arrest he also notified Frank Phillips and Jim McCoy that he would give himself up but preferred to do so just before the trial. Wall acknowledged that while he was confined to the Pike County jail the authorities had allowed him to go about town for several days and that he had held a conversation with "Aunt Sarah McCoy" at the home of Perry Phillips, with Andy Casebolt present. At the time, he declared, Sarah McCoy, in response to questioning, confessed that she had some recollection of Tolbert's telling her at the schoolhouse that Wall had treated her boys with kindness and of his asking her to be kind to "Uncle Wall."

Several witnesses spoke in Wall's defense. Jack Puckett testified that Wall did not get into the line formed at the Reverend Anderson Hatfield's in response to the command of Devil Anse. The minister himself stated that Wall had urged the McCoy boys to go into town immediately after their arrest lest the Hatfields descend upon them and that Randolph McCoy, his son Jim, and one other person had responded that the McCoys had axes and other things to fight with. John C. France remembered Wall's promising that not "a hair on their [McCoy] heads should be hurt here," while Daniel J. Wolford asserted that Wall had stopped Bill Tom Hatfield and others from killing the McCoy brothers on Mate Creek. Finally, John Scott swore that Jim McCoy himself had said that Wall did not have time to get more than "fernent" the place where his brothers were shot.

Frank Phillips testified that he arrested Wall at his home in West Virginia. On the day of the arrest he and Jim McCoy received a letter from Wall stating his willingness to surrender and asking that he not be taken until just before the convening of the court. Phillips, who was then within three miles of Wall's house, ignored the request and made the arrest. Wall accompanied him to the residence of the Mahon brothers.

Phillips stated that he took Wall to the Pike County jail and received the jailer's receipt for him. Following the testimony of Phillips, Andy Casebolt confirmed that he was present when Wall talked with Sarah McCoy and that he remembered her saying that she believed she recalled Tolbert's request that they be considerate of "Uncle Wall."[2]

The jury found Wall guilty and recommended life imprisonment. When the judge refused to grant a motion for a new trial, Wall appealed the verdict on the ground that it was against law and evidence, that the jury had not received proper instructions, and that the jurors had not been kept together after their impanelment. Judge John M. Rice, on September 5, 1889, suspended judgment for sixty days and proceeded with the trials of the other defendants. Alex Messer, Dock Mahon, and Plyant Mahon were tried simultaneously, and all received sentences of life imprisonment.[3]

In addition to the trial of those indicted in 1882 for the murder of the McCoy brothers, eight of the Hatfields and their friends were indicted on August 24, 1888, for the murder of Alifair McCoy during the attack on the McCoy family on January 1, 1888. They included Cap, Johnse, Robert, and Elliott Hatfield, Ellison Mounts, French Ellis, Charles Gillespie, and Thomas Chambers. Gillespie demanded and received a separate trial. Mounts, however, had already confessed that he killed Alifair and entered a plea of guilty. On September 4 the jury returned a verdict of guilty and recommended the death penalty. Mounts attempted, through W. M. Connolly, his court-appointed attorney, to withdraw his plea of guilty. He contended that he had expected mercy in return for his confession and that the tearful testimony of Sarah McCoy had aroused the "passions and prejudices" of the jury against him "to a degree beyond their natural reasoning powers" and resulted in a more severe penalty. He hoped that a fair and impartial trial would extend his life "until the great and good giver of all lives shall take it away." Judge Rice refused Mounts's request and directed that he be confined to the Pike County jail until December 3, when he should be hanged.[4]

Only one of the defendants in the murder cases made a

statement at the time of sentencing. When Alex Messer heard the judge sentence him to "hard labor for the period of your natural life," he rose and, addressing the bench, declared, "Hit's mighty little work I can do, Jedge. Hain't been able to work none o' any 'count for several years." Messer's plaintive statement injected a note of unintended humor into the grim proceedings of the court, and the judge had to rap for silence.[5]

At five o'clock in the afternoon of September 5, the day sentences were pronounced, three carriages left Pikeville with all the condemned men except Ellison Mounts. Guarded by twenty-five mounted citizens, the procession moved across rugged mountain terrain to Prestonsburg, where Sheriff W. H. Maynard, who was in charge, picked up a rumor that Cap Hatfield and a band of Knox countians might attempt a rescue of the prisoners. Maynard hastened the men on to the town of Richardson and placed them aboard a train on the Chatteroi Railroad. He and three guards, C. T. Yost, Jim McCoy, and Frank Phillips, continued with the prisoners to Ashland, where they entrained, by way of the Chesapeake and Ohio Railway, for Lexington.

At Ashland, Phillips spotted James Vance, the son of the leader of the same name who had met his death at the hands of a Kentucky posse, and made gestures of friendship. The younger Vance, however, carried deep hatred in his heart and would have assaulted Phillips had others not restrained him. Maynard placed Wall Hatfield and Dock and Plyant Mahon, who had been granted appeals, in the Lexington jail and continued on to Frankfort with Alex Messer.[6]

The hopes of the condemned men faded on November 9, 1889, when the Kentucky Court of Appeals rendered its decision. It declared that "to find . . . a more inhuman murder we must leave our civilization and resort to the annals of savage life. It is needless, however, to comment on the enormity of the crime or the helpless condition of the young victims of this murderous band. The law has been enforced in these cases, and in its administration the appellants can truly say the jury inflicting the punishment by imprisonment for life 'had tem-

Hatfield family c1897. *Courtesy of the West Virginia Department of Archives and History. Front:* Tennis Hatfield, Louvisa or Midge Hatfield, Willis Hatfield, "Watch," Devil Anse's coon and bear dog. *Middle:* Mary Hatfield Simpkins Hawes and daughter Louvisa Simpkins, Devil Anse and Levicy Hatfield, Nancy Glenn Hatfield and son Robert, Louisa Hatfield, Cap Hatfield, Coleman Hatfield. *Standing:* Rosada Hatfield, Troy Hatfield, Betty Hatfield, Elias Hatfield, Tom Chafin, Joe D. Hatfield, "Ock" Dameron, Sheppard Hatfield, Levicy Hatfield.

Devil Anse Hatfield
*Courtesy of the West Virginia
Department of Archives and History*

Devil Anse and his wife, Levicy, in later years
Courtesy of the West Virginia Collection,
West Virginia University Library

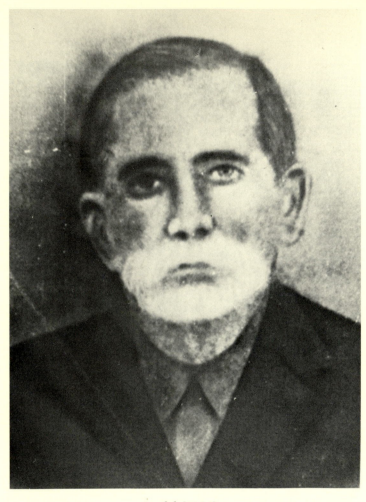

Randolph McCoy
Courtesy of Leonard McCoy and the
Preservation Council of Pike County, Kentucky

Frank Phillips
*Courtesy of Leonard McCoy and the
Preservation Council of Pike County, Kentucky*

Rose Anna McCoy
Courtesy of Leonard McCoy and the
Preservation Council of Pike County, Kentucky

Artist's conception of Sarah McCoy pleading with the Hatfields to spare her sons, August 1882. From *Munsey's Magazine* (1900)

The hanging of Ellison Mounts. *Courtesy of the Pike County Historical Society*

pered justice with mercy.' The judgment of conviction as to each one of the appellants is affirmed."[7]

Ten days later Devil Anse himself appeared in the United States District Court at Charleston, West Virginia, on a moonshine charge, which, strangely enough, had connections with the feud. In May 1889 Dave Stratton went to Charleston and presented evidence to a grand jury which resulted in Devil Anse's indictment. Stratton and some of the detectives hoped to force Devil Anse to make a trip to Charleston and to intercept him en route.

The federal judge, John J. Jackson, Jr., commonly known as the "Iron Judge," recognized the danger which Devil Anse faced. A member of one of the most distinguished families of West Virginia and a relative of Judge William L. Jackson, who proved so effective in Breathitt County, he had a reputation as a choleric, opinionated man. With his arching forehead, deep-sunken and piercing eyes, hooked nose, and long gray whiskers, Jackson represented the very epitome of determination and decision, and his confrontation with Devil Anse promised to be a memorable occasion.

As so often happens, these two strong men of very different backgrounds treated each other with respect. Having no alternative except to summon Devil Anse to Charleston, Jackson sent his chief marshal, Columbus, or "Lum," Sehon, to assure him that he would have protection during his journey not only against his enemies but also against detectives who aspired to capture him. Much to the surprise of many people, Devil Anse received the marshal with courtesy and agreed to appear in court if he could provide his own guard, a condition which the astonished marshal readily accepted.

During his stay in Charleston and the trial Devil Anse found himself treated more as a visiting dignitary than as a man charged with a federal offense. Sehon, keeping his promise, provided a special guard both inside and outside the courtroom, but the Hatfields kept their weapons by their sides at all times, even during the trial. Curious spectators, who came to see the legendary clan leader, found, to their surprise, not an uncouth mountaineer but a benign-looking old man dressed in a navy blue suit, a blue shirt with open collar, and trousers stuffed into the tops of his half-length boots.

Pleased with the attention that he received, Devil Anse gave an interview to a reporter for the *Wheeling Intelligencer*. He began his narrative with his enlistment in the Confederate Army, mentioned his service as leader of a Home Guard unit in which some of the McCoys then allegedly trying to kill him had served under him, and declared that the Hatfield and McCoy families had been good friends until the controversy over the hog. According to the reporter, Devil Anse stated that Ellison Hatfield had sworn out a warrant for Paris and Sam McCoy, who had killed Bill Staton following the incident. Accounts of the relations of Johnse with Rose Anna and Nancy McCoy, the murder of the three McCoy brothers, and other aspects of the feud, however, were at such variance with the facts and with Devil Anse's knowledge of events that one can only surmise that the reporter hopelessly garbled his information.

The close of the trial, which lasted only one day, brought a new excitement, for many spectators knew that both state officials and detectives hoped to capture Devil Anse the moment federal authorities released him. To prevent such a move, Judge Jackson decreed that no state official should lay a hand on Hatfield and directed the federal marshal to provide enough deputies to assure Devil Anse safe conduct until he left the railroad at Logan. Jackson then declared, "When Hatfield gets back to his home, I certainly have no objection to any of you arresting him who may want to try it," a remark which brought a roar of laughter at the expense of the enemies of the patriarch of the Hatfield clan.[8]

Meanwhile, Ellison Mounts, confined to the Pike County jail, granted an interview to a reporter, which appeared in the *Wheeling Intelligencer* on October 21. The reporter found Mounts loquacious and cooperative. He quoted the condemned man as saying, "I don't blame the McCoys. The Hatfields brought me to this." Mounts stated that he saw the three McCoy brothers shot and witnessed the attack on the McCoy family at their home. He insisted, "My guilt was not as great as Alex Messer's, or Wall Hatfield's, or the Whitts', who turned state's evidence." Then, in words that had more of the ring of phrasing of the reporter than of the uneducated Mounts, he complained, "Yet my life pays forfeit, while they are permitted to live. No, I do not look for a commutation of sentence. Nobody seems to be doing anything for me."

Except for the interview with Mounts and the trial of Devil Anse, very little news came out of the feud country. Reports that Julia Ann McCoy and John Hand, a relative of the Hatfields, had been shot at their own wedding proved patently untrue, as did a story that a mob had organized to lynch Sam Mahon, whose illness had resulted in a postponement of his trial. Similarly, efforts of some newspapermen to connect disturbances in Lincoln County, West Virginia, with the Hatfield-McCoy feud lacked credibility. Major J. C. Alderson, who visited Lincoln County in November 1889, declared that all the reports from that quarter were false and that there was no more peaceful locality in the United States. Alderson considered the attempt to relate the alleged troubles there with the Hatfield-McCoy vendetta "absurd." He correctly blamed much of the misinformation and wild rumor on "penny-a-liners at Huntington, Charleston and other points," who had taken advantage of the eastern press and who deserved exposure. He failed to recognize, perhaps, that the Hatfield-McCoy feud had gripped the imagination of the American people and was already on the way to becoming a part of the mythology of the southern Appalachians.[9]

13

THE WAR SPIRIT ABATES

MANY RESIDENTS of both Pike and Logan counties predicted that the Hatfields would never suffer Ellison Mounts to die on the gallows. His execution was originally scheduled for December 3, 1889. Under Kentucky law, however, Mounts automatically had thirty days to file a petition for a rehearing, but he filed no petition. On the evening of December 17 Governor Buckner set the hanging for February 18, 1890. The delays in the execution and the appearance in Pikeville in late January of mysterious strangers, who claimed to be tracing persons illegally cashing checks and horse thieves, strengthened expectations that the Hatfields would attempt to rescue Mounts.[1]

Sheriff Maynard had deep suspicions of Mounts. When, toward the end of January, Mounts refused to talk or eat, his friends insisted that he had lost his mind and that Maynard should summon a jury to determine his sanity. Maynard considered Mounts's behavior a ruse to postpone the hanging and rejected the suggestion. Mounts apparently took no interest in the visits of Dr. J. W. Glover, a physician and pastor of the Methodist Episcopal Church, South, who held services and tried to persuade him to prepare to meet his Maker. On February 17 Mounts expressed a desire to see the scaffold on which he was to be hanged, but the sheriff, fearing another device for a possible escape, refused his request.[2]

Meanwhile, the first hanging in Pikeville in more than forty years attracted crowds estimated at from four to eight thousand persons. Spectators began to arrive on Sunday, February 16, and for the next two days arrived in droves. On the morning of an unusually warm February 18 Frank Phillips provided preliminary excitement. Already intoxicated for the occasion, he staggered about the streets of Pikeville, with a revolver in each hand, proclaiming that he had dealt with the Hatfields and that now he would run Pikeville. Sheriff Maynard failed in his efforts to restrain Phillips, and officers were forced to disarm him. Several of his friends, including Bud McCoy, also intoxicated, then tried to rush the officers and knocked Maynard to the ground. Fortunately, twenty-five militia arrived and restored order.

A few minutes after noon Maynard appeared at the jail with the death warrant for Mounts, who stoically puffed a cigar and blew smoke rings into the air while it was read. After a prayer by the minister, a guard of twenty-four men led Mounts to a waiting wagon, seated him on a coffin box beside Dr. Glover, and conducted him through the town to the waiting scaffold. In accordance with Kentucky law, which forbade public hangings, Pike County authorities had erected a fence around the scaffold, but they circumvented the law by placing the structure at the base of a hill, from which crowds of curious people could obtain a clear view of the execution. They evidently intended that Mounts should serve as an example to others.

When Mounts had taken his place on the scaffold, Deputy Sheriff Weddington asked if he desired to make a statement. Mounts said simply that he was ready to die and that he hoped that his friends would be good men and women and meet him in heaven. His last words, uttered as a black cap was pulled over his head were, "They made me do it! The Hatfields made me do it!"[3]

The hanging of Ellison Mounts produced the inevitable barrage of rumors, many of them ludicrous in the extreme. According to one story, Mounts had lost his mind and the state had hanged a crazy man. Another alleged that the Hatfields had bribed the jail cook to poison the guards in order that Mounts might escape but that the cook had succeeded only in poisoning the jail cat. Yet another reported that the new governor of West Virginia, A. Brooks Fleming, had promised Lee Ferguson that he would honor all requests made by Governor Buckner and would, if necessary, call out the entire State Guard to capture the Hatfields. Fleming flatly denied the report and stated that he had never seen Ferguson. Nevertheless, the *Louisville Courier-Journal* declared that the governor of West Virginia was ready to surrender Devil Anse, Johnse, and Cap Hatfield to Kentucky authorities in return for the delivery of Frank Phillips and Bud McCoy by Governor Buckner.[4]

Perhaps the most exciting of the reports that circulated in the wake of the hanging of Mounts concerned the alleged killing of Frank Phillips by Colonel William O. Smith. According to the story, Phillips met Smith, a former Confederate officer known as "Rebel Bill," who was sawing lumber for the Norfolk and Western Railway, and accused him of killing Phillips's father during the Civil War. When someone subsequently entered Smith's bedroom and tried to kill him, suspicion fell upon Phillips. Although Phillips insisted that he was fifteen miles away at the time of the attack, Smith, so the story went, attempted to serve a warrant on him, and when Phillips resisted, Smith shot him. One version of the story had the killing of Phillips on Peter Creek on April 19 and another placed it on John's Creek on April 20. Some said that the warrant was issued by Governor Buckner, who had honored a request from Governor Fleming for the extradition of Phillips. The excitement subsided when a United States deputy internal revenue collector arrived in Charleston on April 23 with positive evidence that Phillips was alive and Colonel Wallace J. Williamson, who had been attending court in Logan, declared that Smith had been there on both of the days when the alleged killing occurred.[5]

Two events of May 1890 centered around men identified with the Hatfield-McCoy feud. Charles Gillespie escaped from the Pike County jail and made his way to West Virginia, never again to return a prisoner to Pike County, and Dave Stratton, who had reputedly shaken hands with Frank Phillips over the dead body of Jim Vance, met his death. On the morning of May 15 Mrs. Stratton found her husband not far from their house, unconscious and suffering from deep head wounds and a badly bruised chest, from which he died soon afterward. Most people immediately assumed that he had fallen victim to Hatfield vengeance.

Detective W. J. "Kentucky Bill" Napier, who heard of Stratton's death, hurried from Charleston to Brownstown, present Marmet, West Virginia, and swore out warrants for Devil Anse, Cap, Johnse, and Elliott Hatfield and three other men, all charged with complicity in the murder of Stratton. Napier, however, had rushed to conclusions, for it soon became known that Stratton had fallen under the wheels of a Chesapeake and Ohio Railway train while returning home in the dark in a state of intoxication.

Napier himself became the subject of wild rumors. For several weeks after he went to Logan County, nothing was heard of him except a report that he had been seen in Racine, in Boone County, and in Kanawha County. In July the press wires out of Charleston reported that his body had been found within half a mile of a Hatfield home, presumably that of Devil Anse, and that he had a bullet through his heart. About two weeks later, however, a newspaper correspondent in Oceana, Wyoming County, West Virginia, stated that Napier had appeared before a grand jury there in connection with a moonshine case and that, after being assaulted by two friends of the defendants, he had been rescued by local police and then left town.[6]

In contrast to the insatiable demand of the press for news, the Hatfield and McCoy families by 1890 showed signs of becoming weary of the feud. In September the *Huntington Times* reported, "The famous Hatfield-McCoy feud is at an end. After partaking in the bloody butchery of all the men they could kill, after living as outlaws, with prices on their heads, defying arrest and courting meetings with their enemies, after seeing their young men shot down, their old ones murdered, with no good accomplished, they have at last agreed on either side to let the matter rest."

As an evidence of the changed feelings, the *Times* stated, "Two men were seen on our streets yesterday, conversing together in a friendly manner and together taking in the sights of our city. One was a brother-in-law of old man McCoy, the other a son-in-law of Anse Hatfield. They spoke freely of the famous feud, and said that by common consent it would be allowed to cease. Both the parties have gone back to work and are living honest lives without troubling each other. A number of members of both factions are still under indictment for murder and lesser crimes, but will probably now not be troubled by the authorities. West Virginia and Kentucky may both rejoice at the termination of the feud and hope that their annals may never again be stained with a similar occurrence."[7]

Although reports of the end of the feud had circulated periodically for several years, the *Huntington Times* article contained a kernel of truth. In a significant move, Governor Fleming announced that he was withdrawing the rewards offered by West Virginia for the capture of the McCoys. His statement served notice on the Hatfields that the governor's office was abandoning interest in their cause. Without political support, they faced serious disadvantages.

In Pike County, too, support for the feudists eroded. Although the charges against the Hatfields remained on the docket, they excited relatively little interest after 1890. Moreover, two of their strong antagonists had troubles of their own. Lee Ferguson had to defend himself against a charge of stealing government pensions from two Civil War veterans. A. J. Auxier, already accused of being the father of a child born to the wife of another man, was deserted by his own wife, who charged him with "habitual drunkenness" and filed for divorce. The murder of Bud McCoy in late 1890 threatened for a moment to reopen the feud, but when it was discovered that his own relatives, Pleasant McCoy and Bill Dyer, were responsible, the danger of a new outbreak of violence subsided.[8]

The year 1891 brought further hope that the vendetta might be over. On February 24 the Wayne, West Virginia, *Wayne County News* carried an intriguing letter to its editor. It read: "I ask your valuable paper for these few lines. A general amnesty has been declared in the famous Hatfield and McCoy feud, and I wish to say something of the old and the new. I do not wish to keep the old feud alive and I suppose that everybody, like myself, is tired of the names of Hatfield and McCoy, and the 'Border Warfare' in time of peace. The war spirit in me has abated and I sincerely rejoice at the prospect of peace. I have devoted my life to arms. We have undergone a fearful loss of noble lives and valuable property in the struggle. We being, like Adam, not the first transgressors. Now I propose to rest in a spirit of peace." The letter was signed by Cap Hatfield.

Newspaper reaction to Cap Hatfield's letter ranged from cynicism to lavish praise. The *New York Tribune* gave credence to a rumor that on the same day that Cap wrote his letter he purchased two hundred long cartridges. It advised the McCoys to stay on their side of the Tug Fork for a time and "the white-winged dove of peace . . . to fly high in that neighborhood for a while yet." The *Wheeling Intelligencer*, on the other hand, welcomed Cap's announcement and declared, "If Anse Hatfield and his friends had been left alone in peace by the Kentuckians, it is safe to say that the public would have heard the last of the hostilities long ago." Then, violating Cap's appeal to let bygones be bygones, the *Intelligencer* asserted that the blame for the feud rested with the McCoys and that the Hatfields were "honest, thrifty, well-to-do citizens who would not harm a hair upon the head of anyone who had done them no injury."[9]

A report concerning Elias Hatfield in July 1891 provided further confirmation of an abatement of the fighting spirit among the Hatfields and the McCoys. Elias, who served as a special deputy to deliver a prisoner to the West Virginia penitentiary at Moundsville, told a newspaper reporter that members of the two families had not seen each other or, to his knowledge, been within twenty-five miles of each other during the previous two years. Elias berated reporters who had misrepresented events connected with the feud and singled out T. C. Crawford of the *New York World* as one who had grossly distorted them.[10]

The Hatfields and the McCoys, nevertheless, continued to fascinate reporters and their readers. In 1894 the *Williamson New Era* emphatically denied a rumor circulated by raftsmen on the Big Sandy River that Cap Hatfield had been killed by his brother in a poker game and stated that, instead, Cap had become an invalid as a result of an old wound and now professed religion. Another newspaper later declared that Cap had joined the Methodist Church, but it warned the McCoys not to "tempt the saintly convert to fall from grace by presuming too much upon his Christian patience."[11]

If the Hatfields and McCoys had become weary of the fighting, so had most of the residents of the Tug Valley. Eastern Kentucky and West Virginia stood on the threshold of a new industrial era, the excitement of which surpassed the periodic agitation provided by the feudists. By 1890 dozens of representatives of coal and lumber companies had purchased lands or contracted for mineral rights in the Tug Valley. In June 1892 Pikeville installed its first telephone, and some twenty miles away the Norfolk and Western Railway reached Williamson, with construction eventually to be completed to Columbus, Ohio. Frederick J. Kimball, the president of the railroad, declared, however, that the Hatfield Bend of the Tug, "a great sweep of the river, several miles around," was "the worst place on the Ohio extension" of the line and required the construction of a tunnel eight hundred feet long, with a bridge over the river at each end. The company could cope with the engineering problems relating to the tunnel, which was located in the very heart of the feud country, but Kimball encountered "so much lawlessness and shooting that we . . . found it almost impossible to get good men to work."[12] Clearly, by the 1890s the feud was getting in the way of progress.

Political leaders in Kentucky and West Virginia, keenly aware of the demands for a more favorable industrial climate, called for an end to the lawlessness in the mountains. At a statewide development convention held at Wheeling on February 29, 1888, Governor Wilson, who had demonstrated sympathy for the Hatfields, denounced metropolitan newspapers which had sensationalized the Hatfield-McCoy feud. Wilson characterized the notoriety as "bad for the people there [Logan County] and bad for the State, too."[13] The decision of Governor Fleming, Wilson's successor, to withdraw the rewards offered by West Virginia for Frank Phillips and other McCoy partisans was undoubtedly made, in part, with a view to creating conditions more attractive to industry. A wealthy coal baron, who had begun to form connections with the Standard Oil interests, Fleming had little patience with a feud which he considered detrimental to the economic advancement of his state.[14]

William A. MacCorkle, the last of the Bourbon governors of West Virginia, saw the mountain feuds in a different light. Instead of bewailing their adverse effects in discouraging new industry, MacCorkle believed that the advent of industry, improved communications, and an influx of population would stifle the feuds and turn the attention of the people to other matters. He contended that the "discord [in the mountains] . . . was never-ending, because no new life or new blood was brought in to dispel it. A railroad," he declared, "destroys a feud, a manufactory absolutely wipes out neighborhood animosity, and public improvements bring in new conditions." MacCorkle, who had gained an intimate acquaintance with mountain folk while riding the circuit as a lawyer, was convinced that when "any of the civilizing influences of the day came in, the feuds were largely over."[15] The sequence which he envisioned proved substantially correct.

14

THE HABIT
OF VIOLENCE

THE DESIRE OF THE Hatfields and the McCoys for peace could not entirely overcome their habit of resorting to violence in the settlement of disputes. Three incidents are illustrative of the persistence of the tendency to turn to arms. They included the murder of John and Elliott Rutherford and Henderson Chambers by Cap Hatfield and his stepson, Joe Glenn; the slaying of Humphrey E., or Doc, Ellis by Elias Hatfield, the son of Devil Anse; and the killing of Detroit, or Troy, and Elias Hatfield at Boomer, West Virginia. Only the second of the incidents had any relation to the Hatfield-McCoy feud.

The murder of the Rutherfords and Chambers occurred at another of those ill-fated mountain elections, this time in the town of Matewan in November 1896. Cap Hatfield and his fourteen-year-old stepson, Joe Glenn, arrived in town for the occasion, but as an earnest of his peaceful intentions Cap checked his Winchester rifle and other arms with Dr. Jim Rutherford, the mayor of the town. Although Rutherford's daughter Mary had married Floyd McCoy, the son of Randolph, any reopening of the feud seemed unlikely. There remained, however, an old grudge between Cap and the doctor's son John, which had flared up at the election of the previous year.

Throughout the day Cap and John Rutherford kept away from each other, and when Cap and Joe Glenn stopped at the polling place at H. S. White's store on their way home, trouble seemed to have been averted. While they were there, a crowd of men gathered outside. John Rutherford, already far gone with drink, was among them. When Cap and Rutherford saw each other, they almost instinctively opened fire, with no one sure who shot first. Within seconds Rutherford fell, as did his brother-in-law, Henderson Chambers, who had rushed from the store to see what was happening. Cap, seeing Elliott Rutherford, John's nephew, with a revolver in each hand and realizing that his own gun was empty, took cover behind a support for a railroad bridge. Young Glenn, who was concealed behind a large tree, sensed that Rutherford would try to kill Cap. He fired at Rutherford, who also fell to the ground dead.[1]

Almost immediately Sheriff N. J., or Doc, Keadle of Mingo County, which had been formed from the western part of Logan County in 1895, assembled a large posse and began to search for Cap and Glenn. He placed guards along the routes that they might use to escape to Kentucky and had outbound trains searched. A few nights later Detectives J. H. Clark and Dan Christian, who were watching a natural rock fort on Grapevine Creek, which the Hatfields had once used in the feud with the McCoys, spotted their quarry asleep in a crevice. They seized the pair and set off with them at once for the Huntington jail.

One account maintains that when Devil Anse heard of Cap's arrest he gathered about twenty men and started for Mingo County. At the border, however, Keadle and a large posse stopped him and convinced him that any attempt to advance into that county would be futile. Devil Anse recognized then that the force of law rather than the power of the clan would thenceforth rule supreme and bade his men return home.[2]

In April 1897 Cap and Joe Glenn were tried for murder at a special session of the Mingo Circuit Court in Williamson. Although the press resurrected accounts of the Hatfield-McCoy feud, Sheriff Keadle emphasized that the charges on which they were tried were in no way related to the vendetta. The court convicted Cap of involuntary manslaughter and sentenced him to one year in jail. It sentenced young Glenn, who pleaded guilty to the same offense, to one year in the West Virginia Reform School at Pruntytown.

The authorities at the Mingo County jail allowed Cap considerable freedom, and his friends occasionally brought him whiskey. After one especially noisy party in July 1897, Cap made his escape through a large hole cut in the wall with a hatchet. Mingo County authorities, faced with a variety of wild rumors, summoned Devil Anse to Williamson, but he denied any knowledge of his son's escape. Cap soon returned home, and Mingo officials, eager to be rid of a prisoner who had burdened them with the expense of extra guards, left him there.[3]

The following year Humphrey E. Ellis seized Johnse, whom he accused of threatening to kill him, and turned him over to Kentucky authorities. A jury at Prestonsburg found Johnse guilty of several charges, including participation in the murder of the McCoy brothers in 1882 and the attack upon the McCoy family in 1888. Johnse's capture and imprisonment angered the Hatfields, and in July 1899 Elias, the eighteen-year-old son of Devil Anse, sought to even the score. He spotted Ellis, a very popular man, on the rear platform of a train that had just pulled into Gray, in Mingo County. Ellis saw Hatfield and stepped into the coach for his revolver. Anticipating his return, Elias fired at the instant Ellis reappeared and killed him with the first shot. Elias received a jail sentence much too light to satisfy many of the friends of Ellis.[4]

Meanwhile, Governor J. C. W. Beckham of Kentucky repeatedly turned down requests of clemency for Johnse. During one of Beckham's absences, however, Lieutenant Governor William Pryor Thorne granted Johnse a pardon. Sometime earlier, when a burly black had attacked Thorne with a knife during an inspection tour of the prison, Johnse had leaped upon the assailant and saved the lieutenant governor's life. Both the warden of the penitentiary and Thorne considered Johnse worthy of pardon.[5]

Cap, meanwhile, had taken up the study of law during his

time in jail and continued its pursuit for about six months at a law school in Tennessee. Later he passed the West Virginia bar examination and hung out his shingle in Logan. He took little interest in the practice and in later years left the business to his son Coleman and his daughter Aileen, the first woman attorney in Logan County, with whom he formed a partnership. Cap also served as deputy sheriff of Logan County under his brothers, Joseph and Tennis.[6]

Profound changes also began to take place in Devil Anse. More and more frequent became his conversations with William Dyke Garrett, a well-known minister of Logan County, who had fought with the Logan Wildcats before taking up the ministry. At a revival meeting held by "Uncle Dyke" in September 1911, Devil Anse yielded himself to the Lord, and on Saturday, September 23, he was baptized in the waters of Island Creek. Hatfield's profession of faith was the occasion of a "great religious demonstration," but "Uncle Dyke" credited it as much to "the praying and singing Christian people as to me and in the end all the glory is God's."[7]

His conversion, which, according to his neighbors, had left him "much changed," undoubtedly enabled Devil Anse to bear the death of his sons Troy and Elias only three weeks later. Troy and Elias had served as special agents for the Virginian and the Chesapeake and Ohio railroads and had earned reputations for boldness and accuracy with their revolvers. Later they entered the saloon business at Boomer, West Virginia, in partnership with M. J. Simms, a member of the Fayette County Court. Competition from a saloon operated by Carl Hanson at the nearby town of Cannelton cut into their profits. The owners of the saloons agreed to a division of territory, but an Italian, Octavo Gerome, who acted as agent for Hanson, continued to peddle beer and whiskey in the section belonging to the Hatfields. After warning Gerome to stay out, the Hatfields, on October 17, 1911, went to the Italian's house at Harewood, between Boomer and Cannelton. Elias went to the front door and Troy to the back entrance. Observing their approach and fearing serious trouble, Gerome shot Elias and turned upon Troy, killing both. Elias died instantly, but the mortally wounded Troy pumped three bullets into Gerome, any one of which would have proved fatal.[8]

In a spirit of contrition, Devil Anse sought to have the records at Pikeville cleared of the indictments against him and his sons. He sent Joe Glenn, by then a young attorney, to confer with Jim McCoy, the son of Randolph. Glenn offered McCoy ten thousand dollars if he would have the indictments nol-prossed. McCoy assured Glenn that he harbored no hard feelings toward the Hatfields and wished to let the old animosities remain buried, but he declared that he could not consider their offer even if it were for two hundred thousand dollars.[9]

Although Devil Anse and his family adapted to new conditions brought about by the growth of industry, the construction of railroads and highways, and the influx of immigrants, the fighting spirit of the clan and kindred residents of the Tug and Guyandotte valleys continued to erupt occasionally. Beginning in 1919 and continuing into 1921 Logan and Mingo counties experienced severe labor troubles, which grew out of postwar economic readjustments and efforts to unionize the coal mines. During the course of the disturbances Logan County Sheriff Don Chafin, a Hatfield relative, proved one of the staunchest supporters of the coal mine operators. In Matewan, the chief of police, Sidney "Two-Gun Sid" Hatfield, an adopted son of one of the Hatfields, took just as strong a stand for the miners. He became the principal figure in the Matewan Massacre, a battle between miners and Baldwin-Felts mine guards employed by the coal companies, which left nine men dead in the streets of the little town. Hatfield and about twenty other men were charged with murder, but not one was convicted. Among those killed were Anderson C. Hatfield, the son of Deacon Anse and the owner of the hotel at Matewan, and Squire Staton. Later Sid faced new murder charges in McDowell County, West Virginia, this time for "shooting up" the town of Mohawk. Before he was brought to trial, he was "assassinated" on the steps of the courthouse at Welch.[10]

Most of the Hatfields, as well as the McCoys, however, wanted to take advantage of the new ways of living and the opportunities brought with them. Both families produced a respectable number of teachers, businessmen, political figures, and professional men and women. The Hatfields took special pride in Henry Drury Hatfield, the son of Elias and the nephew of Devil Anse, who earned his medical degree at the University of Louisville, served as a surgeon for the Norfolk and Western Railway, and won election to the West Virginia Senate in 1908. He was elected president of the Senate in 1911, and in 1913 he became governor of West Virginia. A progressive Republican, he gave the state an administration marked by significant social legislation and vigorous action, particularly in the settlement of the bloody Paint Creek coal strike of 1912–1913. Devil Anse's own son, Elliott Rutherford, also became a prominent physician in southern West Virginia.[11]

The principal feudists ended their lives in relative quiet. Randolph McCoy spent his last years as the operator of a ferry at Pikeville. His losses at the hands of the Hatfields continued to engross his thoughts, but as the feud receded into history, his tales of woe struck his acquaintances as somewhat boring. He died on March 28, 1914, at the age of eighty-eight, of burns suffered when he fell into an open fire at the home of a nephew with whom he was living. His wife, Sarah, survived him for several years.[12]

Randolph McCoy's death attracted relatively little attention, but that of Devil Anse Hatfield on January 6, 1921, of pneumonia, received wide newspaper coverage, including a notice in the *New York Times*. During his last years he appeared very much the prosperous farmer, who supplemented his income with timbering activities and royalties from mineral properties. His house on Island Creek underwent improvements, including weatherboarding and a front porch, but he never failed in his well-known hospitality. During his last years he refused to dwell on the feud or to talk about it. His funeral, held on the Sunday following his death, was the largest ever held in Logan County and drew several thousand people, some arriving from Logan by special train. Mourners, some of whom bore the name of McCoy, entered the house through a back door and filed through a hallway to the front porch, where Devil Anse lay in a golden oak casket. There was no funeral sermon, but the Reverend Green McNeely, the "scriptural son" of Uncle Dyke Garrett, read commitment rites, and Garrett led in prayers, after which the mourners made their way through a chilling rain to the cemetery. Later the family erected a life-size marble statue made in Carrara, Italy, over the grave.[13]

The following year Johnse died of a heart attack while riding a horse. Cap died in 1930, reportedly of a brain tumor, but an autopsy is said to have indicated that his death resulted from complications from an old bullet wound. Levicy Hatfield, the wife of Devil Anse, followed her husband in 1929. Jim McCoy, the son of Randolph, died in 1929 in his eightieth year of a lingering illness. Serving in his later years as sheriff of Pike County and as a policeman in Pikeville, he was widely respected and regarded as "a good neighbor."[14]

In 1928, forty years after the New Year's attack upon the McCoy family, Tennis Hatfield, the youngest son of Devil Anse, was sitting on the porch of a friend in Pikeville, when he saw an elderly man walking down the street. Tennis asked who the man was. Joseph Stanley, the Pike County jailer, replied that the old gentleman was "Uncle Jim" McCoy. Tennis, then sheriff of Logan County, went over to McCoy, declaring, "I'm Tennis Hatfield, Uncle Jim." He extended his hand, which McCoy grasped with warmth and appreciation. Afterward, the two men, along with three friends, had their picture taken together. By then the Hatfield-McCoy feud lingered on only as a tragedy best forgotten and as the most famous vendetta of the southern mountains.

Epilogue

THE FEUDS THAT ERUPTED in the southern Appalachian Mountains in the late nineteenth century have long since receded into history and are but slightly known to most Americans today. The Hatfield-McCoy vendetta has proved a striking exception and has, in fact, become a part of the folk history of the nation. Many of the feuds had political overtones, but the Hatfield-McCoy troubles were rooted in the everyday life of two families who were essentially no different from thousands of others in the southern mountains. Antagonisms born of wartime emotions, anger over relatively trivial incidents such as the alleged theft of a hog, election-day disputes brought on by overdrinking, and family disapproval of the romantic attachments of some member were the kinds of experiences that were shared and understood by countless Americans.

Although many of its principal events grew out of ordinary situations, the Hatfield-McCoy feud, more than most others, contained all the ingredients of high drama. The persistence of ancient grudges, the total devotion to the clan, the determination that no wrong should remain unavenged, the thirst for blood by high-spirited sons of the hills, and defiance of the law had striking counterparts in the colorful novels of R. D. Blackmore and the history of the Scottish Highlands. Moreover, the chief participants in the feud stand etched in bold relief. Who can forget the patriarchal Devil Anse Hatfield, determined to kill, if necessary, to defend his family and his rights, yet often recoiling at the spreading bloodshed and finally bowing to the simple demands of Christianity? Or Randolph and Sarah McCoy, who lost three sons to a merciless foe in a night of unrestrained revenge? Or the aging Sarah

McCoy, stunned and bleeding, dragging herself along the ground on a freezing January night to save a dying daughter? Or the unfortunate Rose Anna, spurned by Johnse Hatfield, rejected by her family, and dying because she lost the will to live? Such characters seize the imagination and remain unforgettable.

Inevitably, large metropolitan newspapers made the most of the drama that unfolded in the Tug Valley. Correspondents from New York, Cincinnati, and Louisville descended upon the area and provided detailed accounts to their readers. Their reports, often more sensational than accurate, shaped an image of the Appalachian feudists that gained a powerful hold upon pliable American minds. Missionaries, educators, sociologists, and local color writers also discovered the southern Appalachians, which they saw as a region unique and distressingly in need of change. Many of them found the blood feuds peculiarly fascinating and contributed their own interpretations to their causes and events. Still later, dime novelists, motion picture producers, and television programmers found in the feuds source materials for exciting drama. The Hatfield-McCoy feud, more than any other, served as their inspiration.

With such widespread interest in it, it is ironic, but not surprising, that the Hatfield-McCoy feud has become more encrusted with myth and half-truths than any other southern mountain vendetta. Yet, its human and dramatic qualities need no embellishment. Moreover, the character of the people involved, the geographical and physiographical restraints upon them, the stern demands of a frontier environment, the bitterness and suspicion engendered by the Civil War, the weakness of law enforcement, the scarcity of schools and churches, and the powerful influence of the family and the clan, all of which had their impact, give the feud the character of a social and cultural phenomenon. When all the contributing factors are given proper attention, the study of the feud becomes instructive as well as exciting. As history or as drama, the Hatfield-McCoy feud will unquestionably retain its primacy as the best-known and most interesting of all American family vendettas.

Notes

Chapter 1

1. See, for example, *Charleston* (W.Va.) *Gazette*, June 30, 1977.

2. For Hatfield genealogy, I have relied on G. Elliott Hatfield, *The Hatfields* (Stanfield, Ky., 1974), pp. 15–22, 183–200. I have generally referred to Anderson Hatfield as "Devil Anse," a nickname that, despite the uncertainty of its origin, was commonly used during his lifetime and has since become a standard appellation. For its origins, see ibid., p. x.

3. The best genealogy of the McCoy family is Truda Williams McCoy, *The McCoys: Their Story* (Pikeville, Ky., 1976), pp. 235–330. For the McCoy lands on Blackberry Fork, see Pike County Deed Books E, pp. 326–27; L, pp. 202–3; and 5, p. 478, Pike County Courthouse, Pikeville, Ky.

4. William Ely, *The Big Sandy Valley: A History of the People and Country from the Earliest Settlement to the Present Time* (Catlettsburg, Ky., 1887), p. 202.

5. McCoy, *The McCoys*, p. 3.

6. Ely, *Big Sandy Valley*, p. 203.

7. Typical McCoy properties are listed in note 3. For Hatfield lands, see, for instance, Logan County Land Book, 1886–1872, passim, Logan County Courthouse, Logan, W.Va. On March 23, 1877, Devil Anse traded Perry A. Cline a tract of land in Pike County for 5,000 acres on the West Virginia side of the Tug Fork. Logan County Deed Book G, p. 538, Logan County Courthouse.

8. For bootlegging activities, see *The State* [W.Va.] v. *Anderson Hatfield*, Logan County Law Order Book A (1868–1875), p. 68, Logan County Courthouse.

9. T. C. Crawford, *An American Vendetta* (New York, 1889), reprinted in *West Virginia Heritage*, comp. and ed. Jim Comstock and Bronson McClung (Richwood, W.Va., 1969), 3:27. A description of the McCoy house may be gleaned from the testimony of Sarah McCoy, *Commonwealth of Kentucky* v. *Ellison Mounts*, Case

#19602, Kentucky Court of Appeals, Division of Archives and Records, Frankfort.

10. West Virginia, *Biennial Report of the State Superintendent of Free Schools . . . 1881 and 1882* (Wheeling, 1882), p. 67; West Virginia, *Biennial Report of the State Superintendent of Free Schools . . . 1889 and 1890* (Charleston, 1890), p. 76.

11. Coleman Hatfield, "The Feuding Hatfields," p. 121, typescript, West Virginia Collection, West Virginia University Library, Morgantown.

12. Kentucky, *Report of the Superintendent of Public Instruction . . . 1881–1886* (Frankfort, 1886), p. 22.

13. Crawford, *An American Vendetta*, p. 32.

14. McCoy, *The McCoys*, p. 19.

15. Quoted materials are from John C. Campbell, *The Southern Highlander and His Homeland* (New York, 1921; Lexington, Ky., 1969), p. 138.

16. Ibid.

17. Ibid., pp. 124–26.

Chapter 2

1. Virgil Carrington Jones, *The Hatfields and the McCoys* (Chapel Hill, N.C., 1948), pp. 249, 280.

2. Records of Confederate Soldiers Who Served in Organizations from Virginia: Forty-fifth Battalion, Infantry. Microcopy No. 324, Roll 891. National Archives, Washington, D.C.

3. Ibid.; Jones, *Hatfields and McCoys*, p. 272.

4. *Wheeling Intelligencer*, November 22, 1889.

5. *Asa P. McCoy* v. *Henry Davis, Ellison Hatfield, et al.*, File #2589, Pike County Circuit Court Records, Special Collections, University of Kentucky Library, Lexington.

6. *Basil Hatfield* v. *Anderson Runyon, et al.*, File #2049, ibid.

7. *Thomas Hatfield* v. *Joseph Smith, et al.*, File #2038, ibid.

8. *James Lesley* v. *Pleasant McCoy*, File #2606, ibid. See also *Fleming Stafford* v. *James Vance, et al.*, File #2907, ibid.; *Pleasant McCoy* v. *Randolph and Sarah McCoy*, File #1945, ibid., which charges Randolph and Sarah with malicious gossip.

9. Harmon McCoy's military record is noted in Kentucky, *Report of the Adjutant General . . .*, vol. 2, *1861–1866* (Frankfort, 1867), p. 450. For details of Harmon's death, I have generally relied on

128

McCoy, *The McCoys*, pp. 4–11, 221–22. A variant version is Hatfield, "The Feuding Hatfields," pp. 9–14.

10. Versions of the conflict regarding the hog may be found in McCoy, *The McCoys*, pp. 13–19; Hatfield, *The Hatfields*, pp. 24–27; Jones, *Hatfields and McCoys*, pp. 17–24. Contrary to an assertion by Jones, Randolph McCoy and Floyd Hatfield were not brothers-in-law. See McCoy, *The McCoys*, p. 222.

11. Accounts of the trouble between the McCoys and Bill Staton, with the usual variations, are contained in Jones, *Hatfields and McCoys*, pp. 21–23; McCoy, *The McCoys*, pp. 20–24; Hatfield, *The Hatfields*, pp. 28–32. See also Crawford, *An American Vendetta*, pp. 13–14.

Chapter 3

1. Typical of the indictments against the Hatfields are those in Pike County Order Books L, pp. 204, 397, and N, p. 528, Pike County Courthouse. For the armed bands, see Simon B. Buckner to E. Willis Wilson, January 30, 1888, in *Correspondence between the Governors of Kentucky and West Virginia*, Kentucky, Legislative Document No. 2 (Frankfort, 1888), pp. 2, 11; hereinafter cited as Kentucky Legislative Document No. 2; *Louisville Courier-Journal*, February 11, 1888.

2. Diverse accounts of events at the election are in Jones, *Hatfields and McCoys*, pp. 34–36; McCoy, *The McCoys*, pp. 25–34; Hatfield, *The Hatfields*, pp. 33–41.

3. Hatfield, *The Hatfields*, p. 34.

4. McCoy, *The McCoys*, pp. 35–36, states that John Hatfield served as Randolph's emissary to Rose Anna. Jones, *Hatfields and McCoys*, p. 37, errs in referring to Josephine as a younger sister of Rose Anna. Actually, she was nine years older and probably married at the time that Rose Anna was with the Hatfields. McCoy, *The McCoys*, pp. 308–11.

5. *Louisville Courier-Journal*, February 17, 1888; *Wheeling Intelligencer*, February 18, 1888; Interviews with Cap Hatfield, November 11, 1929, and Dr. Elliott R. Hatfield, November 13, 1929, John L. Spivak Papers, West Virginia Collection, West Virginia University Library.

6. McCoy, *The McCoys*, pp. 52, 224; Interview with Cap Hatfield, November 11, 1929, Spivak Papers; Hatfield, *The Hatfields*, p. 68; Jones, *Hatfields and McCoys*, pp. 38, 274.

7. *Commonwealth of Kentucky* v. *Anderson Hatfield, et al.*, Case #19601, Kentucky Court of Appeals, particularly testimony of the Reverend Anderson Hatfield.

8. Ibid., particularly testimony of Randolph McCoy, Sarah McCoy, James McCoy, Joe Davis, Dan Whitt, Jeff Whitt, Plyant Mahon, Dock Mahon, and Ellison Mounts.

9. Jones, *Hatfields and McCoys*, p. 56.

10. Ibid., p. 57.

11. *Commonwealth of Kentucky* v. *Anderson Hatfield, et al.*, File #19601, Kentucky Court of Appeals.

12. Jones, *Hatfields and McCoys*, p. 59.

Chapter 4

1. The description of Cline is in *Louisville Courier-Journal*, March 17, 1888.

2. Ibid., February 18, 1890; *Pittsburgh Times*, February 1, 1888.

3. Jones, *Hatfields and McCoys*, pp. 70–72.

4. Ibid., pp. 73–76. For variant accounts, which name Nancy Daniels's mother as the second victim of the whipping, see McCoy, *The McCoys*, pp. 114–15; Hatfield, *The Hatfields*, p. 74.

5. *Pittsburgh Times*, February 1, 1888; *Louisville Courier-Journal*, February 17, 1888; Jones, *Hatfields and McCoys*, pp. 76–78.

6. Anderson Hatfield to P[erry] A. Cline, December 26, 1886. Copy in Special Collections, University of Kentucky Library.

Chapter 5

1. Hambleton Tapp and James C. Klotter, *Kentucky: Decades of Discord, 1865–1900* (Frankfort, 1977), pp. 386–87.

2. *New York Times*, January 26, 1888; *Wheeling Register*, March 25, 1888.

3. Charles G. Mutzenberg, *Kentucky's Famous Feuds and Tragedies* (New York, 1917), pp. 254–324; Thomas D. Clark, *Kentucky: Land of Contrast* (New York, 1968), pp. 207–33.

4. Mutzenberg, *Kentucky's Famous Feuds and Tragedies*, pp. 187–253.

5. Ibid., pp. 111–86; *Louisville Courier-Journal*, February 17, 1888. For an official and somewhat analytical account of the troubles in Rowan County, see *Special Reports on Rowan County Affairs, by*

Sam E. Hill, *Adjutant General, and Captain Ernest MacPherson, to the Governor of Kentucky*, Legislative Document No. 23 (Frankfort, 1887), pp. 1–23; *Majority and Minority Reports and Testimony Taken by the Rowan County Investigating Committee, Made to the General Assembly of Kentucky, March 16th, 1888*, Kentucky, Legislative Document No. 3 (Frankfort, 1888), pp. 1–551.

6. *Louisville Courier-Journal*, February 9, 10, 17, 1888.

7. Ibid., February 14, 15, 16, 1888.

8. Kentucky, *Journal of the Regular Session of the Senate of the Commonwealth of Kentucky . . .* [1887–1888], (Frankfort, 1888), pp. 908–14.

9. *Louisville Courier-Journal*, August 7, 1885.

10. Ibid., November 30, 1885.

Chapter 6

1. *Wheeling Intelligencer*, February 2, 1888.

2. For differing accounts of the capture of Wallace and the death of Jeff McCoy, see Mutzenberg, *Kentucky's Famous Feuds and Tragedies*, pp. 52–56; Hatfield, *The Hatfields*, pp. 74–77; McCoy, *The McCoys*, pp. 119–27; Jones, *Hatfields and McCoys*, pp. 76–78.

3. *Wheeling Register*, April 22, 1888.

4. Buckner to Wilson, January 30, 1888, Kentucky Legislative Document No. 2, pp. 2, 11. See also *Louisville Courier-Journal*, February 11, 1888.

5. *Louisville Courier-Journal*, February 7, 1888; McCoy, *The McCoys*, pp. 213–14, 227.

6. Wilson to Buckner, September 30, 1887, Kentucky Legislative Document No. 2, pp. 1–2; Buckner to Wilson, January 9, 1888, ibid., pp. 2–3; Buckner to Wilson, January 30, 1888, ibid., pp. 11–12; *Louisville Courier-Journal*, February 11, 1888.

7. *New York Times*, January 29, 1888; *Wheeling Register*, April 22, 1888; Jones, *Hatfields and McCoys*, pp. 87–88.

8. Cline's letter is printed in *Wheeling Intelligencer*, April 24, 1888.

9. Walker to Cline, November 21, 1887, Kentucky Legislative Document No. 2, p. 21.

10. Buckner to Wilson, January 30, 1888, ibid., p. 15; *Louisville Courier-Journal*, February 18, 1890.

11. Phillips to Wilson, December 13, 1887, Kentucky Legislative Document No. 2, p. 8; Wilson to Buckner, January 21, 1888, with

affidavits of G. W. Pinson, Johnse Hatfield, and A. J. Auxier, ibid., pp. 3–6; *Wheeling Register*, April 22, 1888; Jones, *Hatfields and McCoys*, p. 89.

12. *Wheeling Intelligencer*, January 27, April 24, 1888; *Louisville Courier-Journal*, March 6, 1888.

13. Quoted in Jones, *Hatfields and McCoys*, p. 92.

Chapter 7

1. *Louisville Courier-Journal*, February 18, 1890; Testimony of Ellison Mounts, *Commonwealth of Kentucky* v. *Plyant Mayhorn* [Mahon], Case #19601, Kentucky Court of Appeals.

2. For the members of the Hatfield party, see statements of Charles Gillespie, *Cincinnati Enquirer*, October 14, 1888, and *Wheeling Intelligencer*, October 17, 1888, and of Ellison Mounts, *Louisville Courier-Journal*, February 18, 1890. Vance's words are noted in Jones, *Hatfields and McCoys*, p. 95.

3. Jones, *Hatfields and McCoys*, pp. 95–96.

4. For details of the attack upon the McCoy home, I have drawn primarily from the confession of Charles Gillespie, *Cincinnati Enquirer*, October 14, 1888, and *Wheeling Intelligencer*, October 17, 1888; the testimony of Sarah McCoy in *Commonwealth of Kentucky* v. *Ellison Mounts*, Case #19602, Kentucky Court of Appeals; the confession of Ellison Mounts, *Louisville Courier-Journal*, February 18, 1890; and the account of Charles S. Howell, *Pittsburgh Times*, February 1, 1888.

5. *Louisville Courier-Journal*, February 18, 1890.

6. McCoy, *The McCoys*, p. 148; Jones, *Hatfields and McCoys*, p. 102.

Chapter 8

1. McCoy, *The McCoys*, pp. 149–50.

2. The oaths taken by the Hatfields are noted in Jones, *Hatfields and McCoys*, p. 104. For the blame that fell upon Cap for the death of Alifair, see *Pittsburgh Times*, February 1, 1888. For the part of Ellison Mounts, see *Cincinnati Enquirer*, October 14, 1888; *Wheeling Intelligencer*, October 17, 1888; Hatfield, *The Hatfields*, p. 108. An account of the bribe is in McCoy, *The McCoys*, pp. 147–48.

3. *Louisville Courier-Journal*, February 17, 1888; *Big Sandy News* (Louisa, Ky.), January 12, 19, 1888; *Pittsburgh Times*, February 1, 1888.

4. *Cincinnati Enquirer*, January 24, 30, 1888; *Wheeling Intelligencer*, January 25, 1888; *Louisville Courier-Journal*, January 25, 1888; *Pittsburgh Times*, February 1, 1888; Hatfield, *The Hatfields*, pp. 119–29.

5. *Wheeling Intelligencer*, January 25, 1888; *Cincinnati Enquirer*, January 30, 1888; extracts of letter of John A. Sheppard in Wilson to Buckner, January 21, 1888, Kentucky Legislative Document No. 2, pp. 7–8.

6. *Big Sandy News*, January 19, 1888; *Louisville Courier-Journal*, January 28, 1888; *Cincinnati Enquirer*, February 1, 1888; *Pittsburgh Times*, February 1, 1888.

7. McCoy, *The McCoys*, pp. 157–65, 229.

8. Ibid., pp. 166–71, 230.

9. *Cincinnati Enquirer*, January 24, 1888; *Louisville Courier-Journal*, January 25, 1888; *Wheeling Intelligencer*, January 25, 1888; Jones, *Hatfields and McCoys*, p. 111.

10. *Wheeling Intelligencer*, January 30, 1888; *New York Times*, January 29, 1888; Wilson to Buckner, January 26, 1888, Kentucky Legislative Document No. 2, pp. 9–10.

11. *Charleston Daily Star* (St. Albans, W.Va.), January 26, 1888, quoted in Jones, *Hatfields and McCoys*, p. 112.

12. *Wheeling Intelligencer*, January 27, 1888.

13. Ibid.

Chapter 9

1. Buckner to Wilson, January 9, 1888, Kentucky Legislative Document No. 2, pp. 2–3.

2. Wilson to Buckner, January 21, 1888, ibid., pp. 3–4.

3. Wilson to Buckner, January 26, 1888, ibid., pp. 9–10.

4. Buckner to Wilson, January 30, 1888, ibid., p. 10; *Cincinnati Enquirer*, January 31, 1888.

5. *Wheeling Intelligencer*, January 30, 31, 1888; *Louisville Courier-Journal*, January 29, 30, 1888. In West Virginia, the Kanawha Riflemen, as well as the Auburn and Goff Guards, volunteered for action. Kentucky placed the Lexington Guards on the alert. See also Jones, *Hatfields and McCoys*, p. 118.

6. *Cincinnati Enquirer,* January 31, February 1, 1888.

7. *Louisville Courier-Journal,* February 7, 1888; *Cincinnati Enquirer,* February 7, 1888.

8. Buckner to Wilson, January 30, 1888, Kentucky Legislative Document No. 2, pp. 11–17.

9. *Louisville Courier-Journal,* February 2, 3, 1888; *Wheeling Intelligencer,* February 6, 1888.

10. For Caldwell's alleged advice to Wilson, see *Wheeling Intelligencer,* April 17, 1888. Gibson's presentation to Judge Barr and Kentucky's response appear in ibid., February 9, 1888; *Louisville Courier-Journal,* February 9, 10, 1888.

11. *Cincinnati Enquirer,* February 11, 1888; *Huntington* (W.Va.) *Advertiser,* February 18, 1888.

Chapter 10

1. *Louisville Courier-Journal*, February 17, 1888.

2. Ibid.

3. *Wheeling Intelligencer*, February 18, 1888.

4. *Louisville Courier-Journal*, February 28, 29, 1888.

5. Ibid., March 3, 4, 1888.

6. Ibid., March 6, 1888; *Cincinnati Enquirer*, March 6, 1888.

7. *Louisville Courier-Journal*, March 15, 17, 1888.

8. Ibid., March 17, 1888.

9. Ibid., April 6, 7, 1888.

10. *Wheeling Register*, April 17, 19, 22, 25, 1888; *Wheeling Intelligencer*, April 17, 24, 1888.

11. *Wheeling Intelligencer*, April 24, 1888.

12. Ibid., May 15, 1888; *Wheeling Register*, May 12, 15, 1888.

13. *Wheeling Intelligencer*, May 19, 1888; *Huntington Advertiser*, June 30, 1888.

Chapter 11

1. Logan County Land Book, 1887–1892. See specifically the list for 1889.

2. Jones, *Hatfields and McCoys*, pp. 137–38.

3. Crawford, *An American Vendetta*, p. 35; Jones, *Hatfields and McCoys*, p. 138.

4. For the arms purchases, see, for instance, *Cincinnati Enquirer*, January 31, 1888; Jones, *Hatfields and McCoys*, p. 139.

5. *Wheeling Intelligencer*, June 29, August 4, 1888. For the rewards, see *Huntington Advertiser*, June 16, 1888.

6. Quoted in Jones, *Hatfields and McCoys*, pp. 136–37. The *Cincinnati Enquirer*, October 7, 1888, carried a dispatch from Charleston that a McCoy leader had sent word to the Hatfields to "Kill every d----d detective they can find" on the West Virginia side of the Tug Fork and the McCoys would do the same on the Kentucky side.

7. *Wheeling Intelligencer*, June 29, 1888.

8. Interview with Dr. Elliott R. Hatfield, November 13, 1929, Spivak Papers; Jones, *Hatfields and McCoys*, p. 140.

9. *Wheeling Register*, June 26, 1888. The Gibson fight is noted in *Wheeling Intelligencer*, July 27, 1888.

10. For rumor of the flight of the Hatfield partisans, see *Wheeling Register*, August 4, 1888; *Pittsburgh Times*, October 16, 1888; Jones, *Hatfields and McCoys*, pp. 140–41.

11. Jones, *Hatfields and McCoys*, pp. 141–42.

12. Ibid., p. 141. Quoted material is from ibid., pp. 156–57.

13. Crawford, *An American Vendetta*, pp. 24, 26.

14. Ibid., pp. 26–31.

15. *Pittsburgh Times*, October 16, 1888; *Wheeling Intelligencer*, October 17, 1888.

16. *Wheeling Register*, November 18, 1888. For Messer's killings, see also *Huntington Advertiser*, September 11, 1888.

17. Jones, *Hatfields and McCoys*, pp. 157–58.

18. Ibid., p. 158.

19. Ibid., pp. 198–99.

Chapter 12

1. Testimony of Ellison Mounts, *Commonwealth of Kentucky* v. *Plyant Mayhorn* [Mahon], *et al.*, Case #19601, Kentucky Court of Appeals; Jones, *Hatfields and McCoys*, pp. 159–60.

2. Testimony of witnesses cited is in *Commonwealth of Kentucky* v. *Valentine Hatfield*, Case #19594, Kentucky Court of Appeals.

3. Ibid.; *Huntington Advertiser*, September 11, 1889.

4. *Commonwealth of Kentucky* v. *Ellison Mounts*, Case #19602, Kentucky Court of Appeals.

5. *Louisville Courier-Journal*, February 18, 1890.

6. Jones, *Hatfields and McCoys*, pp. 163–64.

7. Ibid., p. 166.

8. *Wheeling Intelligencer*, November 21, 23, 1889.

9. For the Brumfield-McCoy War, as the Lincoln County disturbances were called, see, for example, *Huntington Daily Advertiser*, November 2, 1889. Alderson's report is in ibid., November 26, 1889. The alleged McCoy-Hand killing is noted in Jones, *Hatfields and McCoys*, p. 164.

Chapter 13

1. Jones, *Hatfields and McCoys*, pp. 174–75.

2. *Louisville Courier-Journal*, February 18, 1890.

3. *Cincinnati Enquirer*, February 20, 1890; *Louisville Courier-Journal*, February 19, 1890.

4. Jones, *Hatfields and McCoys*, pp. 180–81.

5. Ibid., pp. 185–86.

6. *Louisville Courier-Journal*, July 12, 1890. See also Jones, *Hatfields and McCoys*, pp. 188–89.

7. *Huntington Times*, September 1890, cited in Jones, *Hatfields and McCoys*, pp. 189–90.

8. Jones, *Hatfields and McCoys*, p. 190.

9. *New York Tribune*, February 1891, and *Wheeling Intelligencer*, February 1891, cited in ibid., pp. 192–93.

10. Jones, *Hatfields and McCoys*, pp. 195–96.

11. *Williamson New Era*, April 1894, cited in ibid., pp. 201–2.

12. Joseph T. Lambie, *From Mine to Market: The History of Coal Transportation on the Norfolk and Western Railway* (New York, 1954), pp. 39–40, 129–31.

13. *Wheeling Intelligencer*, March 1, 1888.

14. Fleming's interests and outlook may be gleaned from John Alexander Williams, *West Virginia and the Captains of Industry* (Morgantown, W.Va., 1976), pp. 138–39, 249–50, passim.

15. William Alexander MacCorkle, *The Recollections of Fifty Years* (New York, 1928), pp. 285–86. MacCorkle, incidentally, remembered the support given him in his candidacy for the governorship of West Virginia by Devil Anse, who was the "controlling influence" in his district of Logan County. After proposing that the Logan County Democratic convention instruct its delegates to support MacCorkle in the state convention and meeting with no success, Devil Anse addressed the Logan countians. "My fellow citizens," he declared, "I have proposed instructions for MacCorkle, and you have not passed them, and you have broken up the convention two or three times, and I will say that if you don't pass them this next time,

Brother Toler and I will go over to my house and get our Winchesters and we will see justice is done." MacCorkle, much gratified by the display of Hatfield decisiveness, received the endorsement of the Logan County convention. Ibid.

Chapter 14

1. For two very different accounts of the triple killing, see *Charleston Daily Gazette*, April 10, 1897, and Jones, *Hatfields and McCoys*, pp. 205–7.

2. *Cincinnati Enquirer*, November 6, 7, 1896; Hatfield, *The Hatfields*, pp. 160–61.

3. Jones, *Hatfields and McCoys*, pp. 210–14. S. S. MacClintock, "The Kentucky Mountains and Their Feuds," *American Journal of Sociology* 7 (October 1901): 184–85, gives the story of an organized effort to apprehend Cap and young Glenn after their escape and of a dramatic battle at the "Devil's Backbone" in which Randolph McCoy allegedly played a conspicuous role. See also Mutzenberg, *Kentucky's Famous Feuds and Tragedies*, pp. 95–108.

4. Jones, *Hatfields and McCoys*, pp. 216–17.

5. Ibid., p. 217.

6. Hatfield, *The Hatfields*, pp. 171–72.

7. *Huntington Advertiser*, October 16, 18, 1911.

8. *Raleigh Register* (Beckley, W.Va.), October 19, 1911; *Huntington Herald-Dispatch*, October 18, 19, 1911; *Huntington Advertiser*, October 18, 1911. For an account by an observer who arrived on the scene within minutes after the shooting, see Interview of Stephen W. Brown with Dave Tamplin of Boomer. W.Va., April 2, 1973, transcript in the possession of the interviewer. A summary of the interview is in *Charleston Gazette*, October 10, 1975.

9. Jones, *Hatfields and McCoys*, p. 229.

10. Charles H. Ambler and Festus P. Summers, *West Virginia: The Mountain State*, 2d ed. (Englewood Cliffs, N.J., 1958), pp. 454–56.

11. Ibid., pp. 381–85; Hatfield, *The Hatfields*, p. 172.

12. McCoy, *The McCoys*, p. 215.

13. *Huntington Advertiser*, January 9, 10, 1921; *Huntington Herald-Dispatch*, January 8, 1921; *New York Times*, January 8, 1921; Jones, *Hatfields and McCoys*, pp. 239–41, 246.

14. Jones, *Hatfields and McCoys*, p. 247.

Bibliographical Note

THE EVENTS of the Hatfield-McCoy feud and the context in which it occurred must be reconstructed from widely scattered sources. There is not a single important body of personal papers. The John L. Spivak Papers in the West Virginia Collection of the West Virginia University Library contain records of interviews with several participants in the feuds, and a copy of one letter from Anderson "Devil Anse" Hatfield to Perry A. Cline is in the Special Collections of the University of Kentucky Library. The West Virginia Collection also contains a typescript, "The Feuding Hatfields," by Coleman Hatfield.

Public archives are of somewhat more value. At the Logan County, West Virginia, Courthouse may be found Logan County Land Books, and those for the years from 1866 through 1892, in particular, shed much light on the holdings of the Hatfield family. There, too, may be found Deed Books B, E, F, G, I, and L, which provide data on Hatfield land transactions, and Law Order Books A and B, which give insights into Hatfield infractions of the law quite apart from the troubles with the McCoys. Pike County, Kentucky, Deed Books B, E, G, L, #2, and #5 shed similar light upon the economic situation of the leading members of the McCoy family.

Of utmost importance in understanding the relations between the Hatfield and McCoy families during the Civil War and through the 1870s are the Pike County Circuit Court Records, now in the Special Collections division of the University of Kentucky Library, as well as Records of Confederate Soldiers Who Served in Organizations from Virginia: Forty-fifth Battalion, Infantry, Microcopy No. 324, Roll No. 891, in the

National Archives, Washington, D.C. Material on the trials of the Hatfields and their partisans in the murders of the McCoys are available in the records of the Kentucky Court of Appeals in the Kentucky Division of Archives and Records, Frankfort. Records of the contests between Kentucky and West Virginia in the United States District Court, the United States Circuit Court, and the United States Supreme Court are in the National Archives, Washington, D.C.

Printed public documents also provide information on the social and cultural milieu in which the feud took place. Useful for the educational climate are West Virginia, *Biennial Report of the State Superintendent of Free Schools . . . 1881 and 1882* (Wheeling, 1882); West Virginia, *Biennial Report of the State Superintendent of Free Schools . . . 1889 and 1890* (Charleston, 1890); and Kentucky, *Report of the Superintendent of Public Instruction . . . 1881–1886* (Frankfort, 1886). Valuable for the lawlessness in eastern Kentucky are Kentucky, *Special Report on Rowan County Affairs, by Sam E. Hill, Adjutant General, and Captain Ernest MacPherson, to the Governor of Kentucky*, Legislative Document No. 23 (Frankfort, 1887); Kentucky, *Majority and Minority Reports and Testimony Taken by the Rowan County Investigating Committee, Made to the General Assembly, March 16th, 1888*, Legislative Document No. 3 (Frankfort, 1888); Kentucky, *Correspondence between the Governors of Kentucky and West Virginia*, Legislative Document No. 2 (Frankfort, 1888); and Kentucky, *Journal of the Regular Session of the Senate of the Commonwealth of Kentucky . . .* [1887–1888] (Frankfort, 1888).

Although they often presented inaccurate and sensational accounts of events related to the feud, newspapers are indispensable to a study of the vendetta, if they are used with discrimination. Particularly useful are the *Louisville Courier-Journal, Cincinnati Enquirer, Wheeling Intelligencer, Wheeling Register, Huntington Times, Huntington Herald-Dispatch, Huntington Advertiser* and *Daily Advertiser, Charleston Daily Gazette* and *Gazette, New York Times, New*

York Tribune, *Pittsburgh Times*, *Big Sandy News* (Louisa, Ky.), and *Williamson* (W.Va.) *New Era*.

Secondary works relating to the feud are legion, but many of them, unfortunately, are thoroughly unreliable. Among the books of special value are such general studies of the southern Appalachians as John C. Campbell, *The Southern Highlander and His Homeland* (New York, 1921; Lexington, Ky., 1969), and Horace Kephart, *Our Southern Highlanders* (New York, 1913), both of which are useful for the culture of the feud country. More specialized, but more antiquarian in approach, is William Ely, *The Big Sandy Valley: A History of the People and Country from the Earliest Settlement to the Present Time* (Catlettsburg, Ky., 1887).

More recent works dealing with Kentucky and West Virginia that contribute to an understanding of the era of the feuds include Thomas D. Clark, *Kentucky: Land of Contrast* (New York, 1968); Hambleton Tapp and James C. Klotter, *Kentucky: Decades of Discord, 1865–1900* (Frankfort, 1977); Charles H. Ambler and Festus P. Summers, *West Virginia: The Mountain State*, 2d ed. (Englewood Cliffs, N.J., 1958); and John Alexander Williams, *West Virginia and the Captains of Industry* (Morgantown, W.Va., 1976). Two works of more restricted nature are William Alexander MacCorkle, *The Recollections of Fifty Years* (New York, 1928), a folksy commentary by a West Virginia governor who was widely acquainted with mountain folk, including some of the feudists, and Arndt M. Stickles, *Simon Bolivar Buckner: Borderland Knight* (Chapel Hill, N.C., 1940), a biography of the governor of Kentucky at the height of the feud.

General works on the feuds of eastern Kentucky include Charles G. Mutzenberg, *Kentucky's Famous Feuds and Tragedies* (New York, 1917), probably the best single volume but not totally satisfactory; Noah and John Reynolds, *History of the Feuds of the Mountain Parts of Eastern Kentucky* (Whitesburg, Ky., n.d.); and L. F. Johnson, *Famous Kentucky Tragedies and Trials* (Lexington, 1972), which deals primarily with the Martin-Tolliver feud. Two articles of some discernment are S. S. MacClintock, "The Kentucky Mountains and Their Feuds," *American Journal of Sociology* 7 (July 1901): 1–28, (October 1901): 171–87, and O. O. Howard, "The Feuds in the Cumberland Mountains," *Independent* 56 (April 7, 1904): 783–88.

Book-length works dealing specifically with the Hatfield-McCoy feud include Virgil Carrington Jones, *The Hatfields and the McCoys* (Chapel Hill, N.C., 1948), the most satisfactory despite its journalistic approach and occasional error; G. Elliott Hatfield, *The Hatfields* (Stanfield, Ky., 1974), which follows Jones's work closely but adds some detail; Truda Williams McCoy, *The McCoys: Their Story* (Pikeville, Ky., 1976), useful for McCoy reminiscences; and T. C. Crawford, *An American Vendetta* (New York, 1889; Richwood, W.Va., 1969), which has the advantage of contemporaneity and detail but reflects a greater desire on the part of its author to obtain a marketable story than to provide an objective study of the feud.

Briefer accounts include L. D. Hatfield, *True Story of the Hatfield and McCoy Feud in the Hills of Kentucky and West Virginia* (Charleston, W.Va., 1944); Shirley Donnelly, *The Hatfield-McCoy Reader* (Parsons, W.Va., 1971); John R. Spears, "The Story of a Mountain Feud," *Munsey's Magazine* (1900): 494–509, and "Two Razorbacks and the South's Biggest Feud," *Literary Digest* 68 (March 12, 1921): 48–55. Finally, a typical version of the feud as it was exploited by the dime novel is W. B. Lawson, *The Hatfield-McCoy Vendetta; or, Shadowing a Hard Crowd*, Log Cabin Library No. 292 (New York, October 18, 1894), pp. 1–29.